SUFI WOMEN OF AMERICA

ANGELS IN THE MAKING

LALEH BAKHTIAR
FOREWORD BY
JAMSHID BAKHTIAR

INSTITUTE OF TRADITIONAL PSYCHOETHICS AND GUIDANCE

© 1996, The Institute of Traditional Psychoethics and Guidance

All rights reserved. No part of this book may be reproduced, stored in a retrieval system, or transmitted, in any form or by any means, electronic, mechanical, photocopying, recording or otherwise, without the prior written permission of the Publisher.

Library of Congress Cataloging in Publication Data

Bakhtiar, Laleh
  Sufi Women of America: Angels in the Making
  I. Mysticism. II. Muslim women. I. Title

ISBN: 1-871031-44-3

Published by
The Institute of Traditional Psychoethics and Guidance
3023 W. Belmont Avenue
Chicago IL 60618

Distributed by
KAZI Publications, Inc.
3023 W. Belmont Avenue
Chicago IL 60618
Tel: 312-267-7001

Contents

Preface — v
Foreword by Jamshid Bakhtiar — vii

Part I: Introduction — 1
What is Sufism? — 3
Women and Sufism — 4
Traditional Psychology — 5
  * Balancing the Natural Three Aspects of Self — 6
  * Disciplining the Animal Energies of
      Lust and Anger — 11
  * Nurturing the Angelic Energy of Reason — 16
  * Attaining Balance — 18
  * Counseling Self to Balance and
      Preventing Imbalance — 18
Profiles of Sufi Women of America — 19

Part II: Awakening — 21
Chapter 1: Accepting Submission to God's Will — 23
Chapter 2: Committing Self to Inner Change — 37

Part III: Consciously Returning to God — 55
Chapter 3: Turning Away From Anything
    Other Than God — 57
  * Avoiding Vices — 57
    Avoiding the Harms of Hypocrisy — 57
    Avoiding Imbalance — 59
      Lust Strong, Anger and Reason Weak — 59
      Anger Rules, Lust, Reason Give Support — 60
      Reason Too Strong or Too Weak — 61
  * Disciplining the Animal Energies Within — 62
    Quantitative Imbalance — 63
    Qualitative Imbalance — 64
  * Sufi Women — 67
  * Holding Animal Energies in Check — 69

Chapter 4: Turning Towards the One God   71
  * Attracting Virtues   71
      From Lust to Temperance   73
      From Anger to Courage   74
      From Reason to Wisdom   75
  * Sufi Women   78
  * Appearance of Angelic Energies (Justice)   82
  * Sufi Women   84

Part IV: Conclusion   91

Notes   98
Bibliography   99
General Index   100

PREFACE
METHODOLOGY

The methodology used in this study was to interview seven Sufi women chosen randomly from the Naqshbandi Sufi Order asking the non-directive question, "How has Sufism changed your life, if at all?" The answers given by them were recorded on tape, transcribed and then compared to the psychology of the 18th century Naqshbandi Sufi saint, Shah Waliullah, as it appears in *Altaf al-Quds* translated as *The Sacred Knowledge*. The translation found here uses the feminine singular rather than the masculine.

Shah Waliullah expounds traditional psychology in this work. It is the thesis of this paper that those who practice a particular discipline need to be compared using the criteria of that discipline, and no other in order to arrive at a fair psychological appraisal. In other words, to do a psychological profile of Sufi women according to Freud or Jung or Skinner's concept of psychology would not be in harmony with what the women interviewed experience because, for these women, the secular world view lacks value and meaning. The method used here is unique but so are the women.

※※※※※

I wish to take this opportunity to thank Shaykh Hisham Kabbani and his wife, Hajji Nazihe, for their encouragement; KAZI Publications for its support; Hoda

Boyer for her excellent editorial comments; and my brother, Dr. Jamshid Bakhtiar, for his foreword.

Foreword

Human beings throughout their existence experience a temporal-personal life journey as well as a timeless-spiritual one. The latter journey is imbedded in archetypal, universal, ethical behaviors espoused throughout human history (the Ten Commandments and so forth). Both journeys are rooted in monotheism.

Sufi Women of America: Angels in the Making is the life stories of women who believe in the monotheistic tradition and practice it. In terms of the timeless-spiritual journey, they are manifestations of the archetypal eternal feminine. At the temporal-personal level, they practice monotheism. As angels in the making, they manifest macrocosmic (spiritual) and microcosmic (temporal) features.

It is important to ask what elements in their development were able to bridge the life cycle of their personal identities with the universal, timeless values that transcended their thoughts and behaviors and represented archetypes of the eternal values that perpetuated a constructive life. The bridge is the esoteric tradition of Islam (Sufism), the Way (*tariqat*), individuation (C. G. Jung), spiritual chivalry (*futuwwah* in Arabic, *javanmardi* in Persian and Urdu). The exposure to this model of consciousness and super consciousness is life saving for individuals, families and society. The timeless journey is specifically spelled out in the life cycle stages of each individual, programmed by the Creator with specific needs, specific goals, specific developmental cycles and specific brain/mind and behavior manifestations that require external cultural, religious, educational, archetypal compasses, templates, inputs for the wayfarer on his/her journey.

The individual is at the mercy of the society and culture of birth. Throughout childhood, without a moral-ethical compass, the person is caught between the deep blue sea and the wild blue yonder with no magnet, no lighthouse to give direction as he/she unfolds throughout the life cycle stages with his/her biological, social and psychological needs unmet, a life disconnected to the Guide (*hadi*)—one of the 99 Most Beautiful Names.

The timeless journey in Islam is represented by the esoteric tradition of Sufism—the battle ground of mind/brain/ and behavior between the spiritual universal values and the "passions" of the soul. While the author has delineated the stations, states and stages of the cosmic journey in her other works, it is the process of individuation (disintegration/re-integration, *fana/baqa*) which is the basis of this present work. Struggling with instinct (passions and reason) and striving toward the divine self (journey to God, in the divine aspect of self and through God) are described in Sufism as disintegration (*fana*) and re-integration (*baqa*).

Disintegration is the giving up of the ego to the divine aspect of self. It is an inner state and outer manifestation of being absorbed in divine action. Re-integration is the spiritual state of living out the attributes of the divine aspect of self from within.

The undoing and decoding of personal life issues and coming to terms with the individuation process or the temporal journey is arduous. It requires faith and courage. It is full of set backs, self-doubts, emotional arousals, cognitive confusions, self-esteem issues and the turmoil of unpredictable behaviors that can be described as a change in the personality—identity crisis and identity diffusion. The personal, temporal journey is to come to terms with past sources of negative-positive inputs in one's life.

This psychological crisis is a preamble to the spiritual journey of universal values and the assuming of the attributes of the divine aspect of self. This is the crisis that determines one's destiny and, through the transcendent function of the mind, establishes the balance between one's personal life history and one's transpersonal, timeless-spiritual life history.

The practice of the Divine Law (*shariat*) and the stages of the spiritual path lead to the state of the Truth (*haqiqat*). The stages of the spiritual path include the learning and practicing of moral-ethical values. As Jesus said, "He who enters not into the angelic kingdom of the heavens and earth is one who has not been born again." The spiritual path is the transformation, rebirth process of the individual in adulthood. Sufi tradition believes the initiated person is born twice: once from his/her mother and once again into the world of love, loving kindness, devotion and unity. Each Sufi order has its own practices to reach the divine aspect within, but all are united in service to humanity—love and monotheism.

These American women are all believers in the principles and practices of Islam. They are women who have experienced life crises and then had access to the esoteric tradition of Islam. In the practice of the greater struggle with the ego at the beginning of the journey to the divine aspect of the self, they take on the ego as a challenge to discover the relationship of the body, mind and spirit or temporal versus timeless values. The journey of this struggle is the cleansing of the mind to come to terms with the instinctive "animal-like" (phylogenetic) wishes, needs, motives and behaviors as it tries to manifest itself during the individual's life (ontogenesis). The person is in turmoil with the instincts, undifferentiated emotions, unreflective behaviors and the need for guidance, re-direction and need for spiritual values, for order, nature and God.

Societies have rituals, laws and institutions to educate and foster human beings to aspire to values that can provide humanity with meaning, purpose and humane existence. Character formation, personhood, self-learning, self-discovery and religious and educational institutions provide opportunities of humanizing and spiritual aligning of the person. The new born child, the developing child, the adult and the elderly need a model of spiritual, timeless order grounded in monotheism and humanization that anticipates the person's biological, psychological, social and spiritual needs/aspirations. The Islamic school of thought is a model—a Guide—that has a perspective of the phylogenetic, ontogenetic and spiritual journey for human beings.

The statistics of human destructiveness, violence, murders, rapes, child abuses, self abuse, neglect, abandonment along with human greed, "I want what I want when I want it," without consideration of other people's needs—that is, human destructiveness without remorse, without a conscience, is rooted in a lack of a moral-ethical container or structure and an emphasis on temporal, personal values where human beings are considered as commodities and where individual lives are more important than humanity's needs.

A school of thought that incorporates spiritual values based on monotheism, based on justice, wisdom, temperance and courage as described in the *God's Will Be Done* series is the greatest source of strength to human beings and prevention of self-inflicted tragedies—the manifestations of rage, anger, selfishness, destructiveness, impulsivity and personal need satisfaction which reigns in the lives of millions of people—the animal instinct—"I want what I want when I want it," at any cost acts as a counter force to reason.

This book and Dr. Bakhtiar's other books are attempts to provide human beings with road maps by presenting a container/structure of values and beliefs to perpetuate a healthy personhood based on timeless values, virtues and role models to serve as guides for suffering humanity— those inflicting the suffering and those suffering. The author, in her writings, formulates the principles of psychoethics rooted in monotheism and presents the Islamic perspective to decrease human suffering and enhance love, kindness and a sense of order in the universe.

Dr. Bakhtiar's presentation of psychoethics and animal drives" has been confirmed by the discoveries of modern brain research. An understanding of the connection will reveal the model of the temporal-personal journey and the timeless journey or the path of the greater struggle.

The functions of the human mind are immersed in the anatomy, physiology and chemistry of the brain. The traditional psychology of Islam has delineated dreams, self-concepts, beliefs, attitudes and virtues in thoughts, feelings and behavior. The attitudes, character, life style and behaviors of individuals have been chronicled and observed by wise people who distinguish behavior in terms of good-bad, vice-virtue, evil-virtuous and destructive-constructive. The Koran and books on ethics along with the teachings of Sufi masters are all attempts to prevent humanity from destroying itself and others.

Phylogenetically and ontogenetically the emotional centers of the brain are located in the limbic system. The reactions and responses arising from the limbic system, without the filtering effect of the neocortex (the thinking, reflecting, comprehending, planning portions of the mind), are instinctive and animal-like, manifested by impulsivity, aggressiveness, rage, fear responses, destructiveness, expression in action without reflection or consideration of pain inflicted on the other person or the self. The limbic system is the brain's center of passion, emotions of lust, fear, rage or so called animal instincts. Whenever human beings are in the midst of craving, intense desire, fury, rage or fear, the limbic system is at work. Automatic responses without reflection is key to limbic system actions. The neocortex super imposed on the limbic system gives human beings thinking, reflecting and monitoring functions (attraction to pleasure and avoidance of pain). The perceiving five incoming senses and added reason to emotions give rise to reflected actions.

The neocortex is used to bring about civilization, culture, long term planning, reflection, consideration of others and development of psychoethics, rules of conduct and recognition of timeless values. The presence of the neocortex and its neurocircutary connectedness with the limbic system and the internal five senses bring about mother-child bonding, long term commitment to child rearing, and family perseverance, commitment to rituals, education and necessity for universal values perpetuating the constructive characteristics of human behavior.

The neocortex and the affective limbic system and memory system of the brain need the input of education, models of conduct, spiritual values and road maps of life's ontogenesis in order to utilize the functions of the brain and give the right responses to the limbic system. Without a formulated input system of ideas, guides, concepts, skills and role models the individual is at the mercy of the limbic system and the output in behavior is consistent with those functions.

The contribution of Dr. Bakhtiar is invaluable for the betterment of human conduct. The era of computer super highways, internet, discovery of new stars and planets millions of light years in space, genetic engineering and the fascination with the outer reality of tools, computers, machines and facts needs a balance in order for the inner self to reach the divine aspect of self and succeed in its struggle. Only in this way can humanity be saved from its own destructiveness. It is the commitment to our own behavior and the cognition of the needs of our children and our families that need reframing and recognition. Schools and institutions are searching for values and attitudes of personhood that are more important than the content of the specific courses being taught.

This present work along with her previous works are a gift to humanity, a humanity that so desperately needs spiritual guidance—timeless, universal values in a system of justice balanced by wisdom, temperance and courage. Dr. Bakhtiar, my biological and spiritual sister, in the formation of the Institute of Traditional Psychoethics and Guidance and her numerous publications, senses the soul-spirit of suffering humanity for order, for love, for balance and for uprooting the roots of human destructiveness. *Sufi Expressions of the Mystic Quest, Ramadan: Motivating Believers to Action* and the three volume work of *God's Will Be Done* are heartfelt guides to imbue our lives with the spiritual values for ourselves, our children and our society in order to prevent destructiveness without remorse.

I am honored to have had this opportunity to write the foreword for the reading public. As a psychiatrist working daily with the healthy functions and dysfunctions of the mind, brain and behavior, I sense, know and feel the absence of moral-ethical healing, of the spirit in our modern strategies to help our fellow human beings.

The Koran states, "Jews and Christians and whoever believes in God and does what is right shall have nothing to fear or regret. God loves not the aggressors. Do not allow your hatred for other people to turn you away from justice. Deal justly. That is nearer to true piety."

I envision families, groups of young children, adolescents, adults and elders working together in community based clusters of people engaged in psychoethics—renewing their faith, seeking piety, compassion, friendship, positive emotions, love, parenting skills, communication skills, self-reflection and problem solving based on timeless spiritual values, reframing shifting paradigms, developing a moral-ethical "report card" for themselves and their communities that is based on love and knowledge. The world population in the past 1000 years has grown from 300 million to near-ly 6 billion. The task of core values, core principles of conduct are essential if humanity is to survive in a healthy constructive manner.

"O dervish, human beings of every nation and religion all exist by the honorable cloak of existence. All are human beings like you. If you are truly a lover of Absolute Being, love all beings and be kind to them. By doing so you prove that you deserve the privilege of belonging to the human family."*

---

* Javad Nurbakhsh, *In the Tavern of Ruins*.

PART I
INTRODUCTION

INTRODUCTION

WHAT IS SUFISM?

Sufism is difficult to define because to many it is much more than an "ism." The purpose of it, however, is clear. It is to purify and edify the self. This purpose has its basis in the Quranic verses, *"He it is Who raised among the inhabitants of Makkah a Messenger from among themselves who recites to them His communications and purifies them ...."* (62:2-3).

Shaykh Muhammad Hisham Kabbani comments on this verse, saying,

> ....One of the principles mentioned in this verse, purification (*tazkiyya*), is described by the words, *"and purifies them."* It means to purify the believers from all kinds of association with God, to purify their hearts and to prepare them for the state of good character. According to Ibn Kathir, *tazkiyya* means "to sanctify," which means to raise the individual from a state of materialism to a state of purification of the heart. The state of good character, which is the second essential component of Sufism, is mentioned in the Traditions of the Prophet. This term is mentioned in the Tradition where Gabriel appeared to the Prophet while the Prophet was sitting among his Companions and questioned the Prophet about the definition of the terms submission to God's will (*islam*), the

beliefs of submitting to God's Will and the way of perfecting character.[1]

Whereas we could quote many more definitions of Sufism and descriptions of its purpose,[2] it is sufficient for us here to recall that Sufism deals with purifying the self of the rust and pollution of earthly, material life and requires a commitment to inner change to succeed.

Sufi literature speaks of the process of self-purification or transformation in many ways. One way of understanding this process is as a journey of return to our true nature originated by God. This is accomplished through turning away from anything other than God (*fana*) and then turning towards God (*baqa*). This is the process upon which traditional psychology is based. Methods of effecting transformation are variously referred to as: self-purification, the process of self-effacement, letting go of our negatively conditioned behavior, controlling ego or animal qualities and enhancing inner angelic qualities through spiritual practices.

The process of putting this belief into practice is Sufism. When Sufis speak of self-purification, they refer to the eradication of worshipping anything but the One God.

The task of processing the knowledge that God is one and successfully living that knowledge in every single thought and deed is an extremely difficult one, the reward of which is the greatest happiness available in life. The Sufi task is to turn away from everything other than the One God, and to return to the spirit within in order to become one with it.

WOMEN AND SUFISM

In regard to understanding Sufi women who have attained self-purification, one of the clearest explanations appears in Dr. Javad Nurbakhsh's prologue in *Sufi Women*. He says:

The question often asked is whether or not there have been any women among the Sufis who attained the station of the perfect human being. In response: Throughout the Quran there are many instances in which God concurrently addresses both women and men believers. The significance of these exhortations is that in terms of their faith, man and woman are equal. For instance, both are often mentioned side by side, *'Men and women who have surrendered, believing men and believing women, obedient men and obedient women, truthful men and truthful women, enduring men and enduring women, humble men and humble women, men and women who give in charity, men who fast and women who fast, men and women who guard their private parts, men and women who remember God often. For them God has prepared forgiveness and a mighty wage'* (33:35).

He continues with the following Tradition,

'God does not look at your forms.' The essential implication of this Tradition is that on the path of ascent toward the Truth, it is the heart's work that ultimately is weighed, not this corporeal form of flesh and blood. Furthermore, all great Sufi masters have held the firm conviction that any woman who engages in the path of divine love is not to be deemed 'female' in the sense of being passive, but rather is to be judged solely by her humanity....

Suffice it to say that women who seriously set foot on the path toward Reality are in exactly the same position as men who do so. Or, to express it somewhat differently, since in the ocean of divine unity neither 'I' nor 'you' exists, what meaning can 'man' or 'woman' have?[3]

TRADITIONAL PSYCHOLOGY

Traditional psychology or psychoethics uses an experiential and phenomenological approach to self-purification. The phenomenological aspect of this approach can be understood by the fact that everything visible or invisible, seen or unseen, is considered to be a Sign of God.

BALANCING THE THREE NATURAL ASPECTS OF SELF

Balancing ourselves comes from disciplining our animal qualities, our passions and nurturing our angelic energies or reasoning abilities according to traditional psychology. When we have succeeded in doing this, we are balanced, centered. The seven women presented here have committed themselves to inner change and are aware of the need for balance. As such, they are angels in the making—that is, women who have disciplined their animal qualities and are, thus, becoming spiritual beings in human form. In order to understand this process, some information about traditional psychology will be helpful.

Animal energies are seen to operate in two different areas within us as the natural tendency to avoid pain (vices) and/or to attract and experience pleasure (virtues). For instance, while we are attracted to the pleasure of eating, we must, at a certain point, turn away from the table in order to avoid the harm of overeating.

The division between avoiding harm and seeking pleasure is an important distinction to make, even artificially, in order to better observe the natural state. This, at least, is the view of traditional psychology which is the basic criterion used here to understand the position of women who commit to inner change. It is this psychology with which they are in tune.

Self-purification, the goal of the commitment to inner change in traditional psychology, is effected when our animal energy of avoidance of harm disciplines our attraction to pleasure. That is, we are attracted to eating, sleeping or sex as natural inclinations in order to survive as a race, but if we forget about what could be harmful in too much or too little food, sleep or sex, we lose our natural state of balance. Our awareness does not stop here, however.

Our awareness of what could be harmful in the

excess or deficiency of a natural inclination needs to be kept in balance by our angelic energies of which reason is but the first sign. While our reasoning function serves as the regulator, it can become too regulatory and demanding or, conversely, it can regulate and order too little. In other words, it also needs to be kept in balance by allowing our animal energies to function.

When a balanced self is the goal, our brain rules over our heart, our heart disciplines our gut and our gut sends filtered messages to our brain. Our brain needs to be the strongest of the three in order to decide whether or not to accept subliminal messages from the gut.

The interaction of the two sources of animal energy, avoidance and attraction, with the balancing angelic energy, should move in a time tested sequence as Shah Waliullah points out. The movement should be to first strengthen that aspect of self—gut, heart or brain—which is the strongest and then to work on the areas that are weaker.

> In many disciples one faculty is by nature very strong while the others are very weak. Now if one blindly begins to carry out exercises with the object of training and refining all the faculties simultaneously, an extremely long time will be required even for the dominant faculty to regain strength, and to manifest signs of the purification necessary to enable the seeker to reach the desired stage. But if the seeker were to strengthen the faculty which is innately strongest and to purify the others only summarily, then the objective could very quickly be achieved and the desired stage reached without delay. The final goal, which is reached after passing through a number of stages and undergoing a number of annihilations, is in fact attained thanks to the faculty which is by nature the strongest.[4]

The terminology can become very confusing and therefore is best clarified at the beginning. Animal energies consist of attraction to pleasure and avoidance of harm. Attraction to pleasure, also called lust, is located in the liver (sometimes called gut) and often referred to as the soul in general terms (*nafs ammarah*). Its natural function is to preserve the species.

Avoidance of harm is located in the heart and is often referred to as anger or the "heart." Its natural function, likewise, is to preserve the species.

Reason is located in the brain and is often referred to as the "intellect." The intellect's natural function is to preserve and nurture the possibility of the return to paradise.

There are three imbalanced possibilities for each of the three functions: too much or too little in terms of quantity or total depravity in terms of quality.

There are three balanced possibilities of each of the three functions as well. A balanced function of preserving the species is called temperance. A balanced function of preserving the individual is called courage, while a balanced function of preserving the possibility of the return to paradise is called wisdom. When these three work in harmony, the person becomes centered. The proof of being centered is the appearance of fairness or justice in the person.

The three kinds of persons then are firstly those in whom the angelic energies or cognitive abilities, located in the brain, are dominant. This type, when balanced, manifests wisdom. The second kind are those oriented to the lustful, pleasure-seeking, species-preserving energies located in the liver or gut. This type, when balanced, manifests temperance. The third group are those characterized by the angry, danger-avoiding, self-preserving energies located in the heart. This type, when balanced by the angelic reasoning energies, manifests courage.

Thus, seekers are cautioned not to go to an extreme in one area of worship, i.e. prayer and fasting, while losing another area of worship, i.e., earning a living and relating to people. Shah Waliullah emphasizes the importance of balance.

God in the Quran has drawn a very vivid picture of these three kinds of persons and has removed the extraneous material which fools had allowed to be mixed with this spiritual method. Thus He prevented people from fasting continuously and frowned on a life of isolation and seclusion. This was in order that the balance should not be lost on the scales of the spiritual method—between internal constitution and the requirements of a healthy nature.[5]

Shah Waliullah speaks in greater detail further clarifying the three possible areas of strength and their interaction with other areas that may be weaker. Here he refers to lust as the soul, anger as the heart and reason as the intellect.

The human faculty may be subdivided into three branches: the soul, the heart and the intellect. All three of these faculties are mentioned in the Traditions of the Prophet Muhammad, peace and the mercy of God be upon him. From this source we are able to gather that desire and the pursuit of pleasure are the attributes of the soul. Forming the intention to carry out a particular action, entertaining feelings of love and hatred, showing courage or cowardice, etc, these are the characteristics of the heart. Understanding and knowledge and the capacity to decide what has to be decided, these are the qualities which are attributed to the intellect.[6]

In summarizing the three major types of people, Shah Waliullah shows the interconnectedness and deep "ecology" of the self.

Unless the soul obeys the heart, the veins of the throat will not swell nor will the spirits be aroused. Unless the intellect displays to the heart the image of some threat, hatred and the desire for revenge cannot arise. Similarly knowledge which is not accompanied by the firm intention of the heart can simply be called "talking to oneself." If a mental perception lacks the conviction which sense perceptions can lend to it, it is bound to be lame and distorted. Likewise the soul without the support of the intellect or the heart is as helpless as a three month old baby. Such a person is unable to muster confidence, firmness and strength from within herself.

Such characteristics as these are like natural bodily needs whose total eradication is absolutely impossible. Lord knows they may be temporarily concealed while severe exercises are being performed, but no sooner are these exercises discontinued than they appear once more. In fact the purification of these characteristics can only consist in this: that one uses them in their proper place, contenting oneself with what is necessary and avoiding excess.[7]

Shah Waliullah then summarizes the location of each of the three-fold aspects of self and describes their balanced state.

To recapitulate briefly: the soul is located in the liver, the heart is located in the physical heart and the intellect is located in the brain. Attraction to pleasure permeates the whole body but is firmly rooted in the liver; the avoidance of harm is present throughout the whole body but it is firmly rooted in the heart and balanced reason also pervades the entire body but it is firmly rooted in the brain.

There are those whose faculty of lust is highly purified. They are thus called the pious and they are entirely engrossed in giving up the charms of this transitory life.

There are those whose faculty of anger is well-purified. They are known as the trustworthy, the martyrs, the worshipping devotees. Friendship with God and with his Prophet and perpetual service have become their dominant characteristics. All their anger is vented in waging war on the enemies of God.

Those whose intellectual faculty and cognition is very

strong are accordingly known as 'those firmly rooted in knowledge'.[8]

DISCIPLINING THE ANIMAL ENERGIES OF LUST AND ANGER

LUST

Shah Waliullah elaborates on the function of the natural state of attraction to pleasure or natural lust at another level.

The basic function of the attraction to pleasure function is to look after the carnal needs and to pursue whatever is pleasurable. In addition it has to maintain the constitution of the body in accordance with the latter's requirements. Hunger and thirst, fatigue, the sexual urge and excretory needs, all of these are connected with the attraction to pleasure and form the absolute necessities for the continuance of life.[9]

Sometimes this natural function in us is very strong while our natural state of avoidance of harm and/or reason may be weak. This state has been compared by the other traditional psychologists to animals other than beasts of prey, but Shah Waliullah likens it to vegetables.

There is a type of person whose natural powers of lust—her digestion, her power to catch and hold, her sexual energy—are all extremely strong, but as far as the qualities of her function of anger and the perceptiveness of reason are concerned, she is nothing but a dull-minded idiot. Anger, courage, fear and shame are slow to appear in her and disappear in no time. Her recollection of the past is extremely feeble as is her capacity to plan for the future and decide what is good or bad. Such a person may be likened to vegetables.[10]

Sometimes one of the three aspects of self is emphasized in the nurturing process and the other two aspects are neglected. This causes imbalance because the interdependency of the parts is thwarted and the natural "ecological" cycle is broken.

If both the natural function of anger and reason are subservient to and weaker than the function of lust, then a great many vices will result. The attraction to pleasure in that state is generally known as lust. Such acts, for example, as indulging in illicit sexual pleasures and/or continuously gazing at and caressing one's beloved, cause the avoidance of harm to follow suit (by weakening resolve). They (the animal energies) arouse an inclination for the loved one and fill the heart with love. At the same time they compel reason (weakened because resolve has been weakened thereby allowing imagination to creep in) to summon up the image and memory of the beloved and to find ways and means to effect a union. All of this is called love. In the same way, indulgence in delicious food and drink causes the avoidance of harm and reason to follow suit. With a little attention such patterns are easily recognized.[11]

The reason for attraction to pleasure to be controlled by avoidance of pain and cognition is then presented by Shah Waliullah. When pleasure-seeking is controlled by them, the conscience can exercise its ability to command what is right and prevent the development of what is wrong. Otherwise, it commands what is wrong leading to imbalance and prevents the development of what is right which leads to balance. This, as we will see, is one of the signs of hypocrisy. When the energies of lust are too strong,

....she is given over to sexual indulgence and eating delicious food. Even though the fear of the punishment meted out for such actions may occur to her, and her intellect may vividly portray the abuse, humiliation and hatred which await her, she is unconscious of what she is doing. All of which makes people of sense realize that every part is busy dominating as well as supporting the other. The intellect may occasionally understand the baseness of the action and its evil consequences, but it cannot put its orders into effect.[12]

If reason prevails over the instinct to anger within the self and the energies of anger dominate over those of natural lust, a balanced state is produced in the individual. She may then proceed to fix the suitable course for her energies of lust to follow in order to satisfy such needs as eating, drinking, clothing, shelter, marriage, etc. in such a way that these do not clash or conflict with her ability to reason nor do they impede her anger functioning. In this manner the reformation of the faculty of lust is achieved. The individual allows her anger to pursue the middle course in life at the same time as avoiding any disturbance of the energies of lust. In this way she cherishes true love for the Almighty—real faith, awe, and hope in God. Clearly reason has an important part to play in both these processes.

Practices have been established by means of which energies of lust can be made to obey both anger and reason. Such practices as the keeping of the prescribed fast and the performance of good acts for the expiation of sins are prescribed. Here both reason and the energies of anger within the self combine to demand the performance of a particular act, whether the function of lust should wish it or not. Similarly a method has been found for the purification of the energies of anger and this consists of perpetual service and the practice of audition.[13]

ANGER

The person characterized by the quality of anger transformed into courage is next described. In this natural, balanced system of psychology, cognition or reason should rule over anger and anger in turn should rule over lust. Shah Waliullah describes the scope of the energies of anger, the irascible faculty, or avoidance of harm when energies of the concupiscent faculty and the intellect are weaker.

The function of avoidance of harm is to show anger, shame, fear, courage, generosity, avarice and hatred. Everyone knows for certain why she dislikes a particular thing, why she struggles with the agitated desire to repel it, why her spirits seem on the point of leaving her body, why her veins dilate and why her skin becomes red. Similarly, in times of fear, she knows what her avoidance of harm resembles. Her spirits seem to retreat within her body, her face becomes pale and her mouth goes dry. It is in this way that the characteristics of the avoidance of harm may be assessed.[14]

When an individual's anger function is too strong while the other functions of lust (or attraction to pleasure) and reasoning ability are too weak, Shah Waliullah compares her to a beast of prey.

Then there is the person of courage and zeal, generosity and authority. In these qualities she surpasses her fellows, but in her natural and intellectual powers she hardly possesses a tenth of what others possess. She is like the wild beasts.[15]

In order to attain balance, the energies of concupiscent lust or attraction to pleasure need to be strengthened along with reason. When there is no balance, the conscience, cannot command what is right and avoid what is wrong. In fact, the opposite occurs and again hypocrisy rears its head.

If both the attraction to pleasure and reason happen to obey the avoidance of harm, a number of different vices will appear. The avoidance of harm in that condition is called the aggressive self. Besides violent anger, a whole array of other vices arise in the aggressive self. For example, if the avoidance of harm has an underlying spirit which is coarse without being evil, then the person in such a state will seek to dominate those around her. This characteristic is innate in the avoidance of harm which is why the attraction to pleasure lends its support. Avoidance of harm summons up fresh strength and rouses the person's inborn spirits to lend assistance. Supposing it is necessary to abstain for a period from eating or drinking or marriage. The heart raises no objections and does not rise in revolt. Reason, too, shares in the action of the avoidance of harm and for its sake hits on many an elegant stratagem and plan for the future.

This person is so strong in her heart that when she becomes angry or jealous or is overtaken by worry or shame, her attraction to pleasure ceases to function. She feels neither hunger nor thirst and lacks even the strength to digest and evacuate. No matter how much her reason may chide her and tell her that there is no point in showing anger or worrying, it is impossible for her to escape the dictates of anger.[16]

When the attraction to pleasure is too weak and avoidance of harm too strong, another situation may result.

It sometimes happens that the attraction to pleasure is filled with desire for a sweetheart and yet the necessary sexual energy is lacking because it is too weak in relation to avoidance of harm. Or the avoidance of harm may be filled with contemptuous and vengeful thoughts and yet the arm is bereft of all strength. Occasionally in such cases the attraction to pleasure comes to the aid of the avoidance of harm and pours in renewed vigor which was lacking before. This vice is also extremely difficult to eradicate and avoid.

Furthermore God allowed avoidance of harm to rule over attraction to pleasure and direct such of its activities as were desirable towards the life to come. As a result it became like someone who relinquished immediate gain in favor of the profit of future life. Basically this method consists in following the natural equilibrium. And so the bodily method is for the body to follow nature while the spiritual method consists in following a strong and balanced self.

To expand on this point: all individuals of whatever species differ from one another. Some manifest the specific form completely while others, owing to inherent physical defects, do not receive every aspect of the inherent imprint. There are even some who are fundamentally at odds with the characteristics of the species. For example, the specific human form requires that sexual desire or lust and anger should appear fully and completely in the human being—not partially. In some people all these are indeed manifested in a complete form but in others they are only partially apparent. There are others yet again in whom physical degeneracy has brought about undue timidity and impotence.

The human being's internal constitution demands that reason should rule over avoidance of harm and the avoidance of harm should discipline the attraction to pleasure.[17]

NURTURING THE ANGELIC ENERGY OF REASON
Reason for traditional psychologists means:

....belief in the existence of God Who sends messengers, reveals scriptures, decrees what is lawful and what unlawful, rewards the deeds of His servants and knows both what is manifest and what is hidden. All this God has done as a reminder of His blessings for the obedient and His punishment for the disobedient and of death and what follows thereafter. He has prescribed actions in keeping with this point of view such as regular prescribed prayer so that when one's conscience is eventually convinced of their benefit, the animal energies will in turn be duly reformed. The individual will experience the fear of punishment, the hope of reward and the love of God in all the Signs.

God bestowed special blessings upon reason so that God might converse with it according to its nature. God gave it a certain degree of freedom in order to enable it to understand

God's attributes and in order to remove its suspicions and doubts. God also bestowed other favors on it such as empowering it to rule over the animal energies and deal with them according to their nature in the light of the fear, hope and love of the Benefactor, retaining those aspects of the nature of self which would be of value in eternity.[18]

Reason, even though the most basic of angelic energies, can be tainted by the animal energies of lust and anger. It then loses its natural inclination towards balance. Shah Waliullah describes an imbalance of reason which is difficult to overcome.

Sometimes reason may absorb knowledge calculated to further the drive for conquest. To this end it then begins to think out beneficial contingencies and effective plans thus retreating from its former convictions. This is a vice which is extremely hard to eradicate.[19]

Shah Waliullah elaborates on the function of reason as cognition or the divine spirit infused at another level.

The function of the intellect is to recollect the things of the past and plan for the things of the future. Again there is the type of person who distinguishes herself from those around her by her capacity to retain what she has heard, and her ability to adopt the right course but she has no share whatsoever in the natural energies of those of the avoidance of harm. Hence she is comparable to the lower angels.

If both the avoidance of harm and the attraction to pleasure are governed by reason, then praiseworthy qualities will result. The soul in this condition is known as the serene self, the self at peace. For example, when a person comes to realize through her intellect that her happiness lies in performing of good actions while bad actions will only bring her misery, then her lust no longer goes against or objects to the command of reason and her heart, too, begins to show love and desire for what reason requires. It often happens that a person of abundant intellect thinks of some desirable worldly or religious objective. Then however much her anger may dislike certain aspects of it. Even though sweet pleasures may meanwhile be slipping through her hands, still her anger and lust do not disobey her reason.[20]

ATTAINING BALANCE

Balance or being centered in the view of traditional psychology is to return to the nature within originated by God (*fitrat Allah*). This nature was actualized at our birth when we were so pure as to be a potential mirror image of the divine spirit within us. Our life is then spent as an inward journey, an attempt to keep that "mirror" polished and free from traits that indicate the presence of other than God.

This inward return journey is fraught with obstacles and barriers brought on by the nurturing process—the environment in which we grew up, the people to whom we related (parents, teachers, relatives, siblings, friends) and the knowledge we experienced. If the totality of these experiences did not reinforce our nature originated by God, then each and every incident acted like a piece of dust or rust on the mirror of the pure self, the mirror of our divinely inspired origin. Over time, that mirror becomes so full of dust or rust that it is no longer able to reflect our original inner God-given nature.

What is this nature originated by God? It is an innate belief in the Oneness of God which at one level manifests as conscience. Conscience is the highest perceptual development that God's Will—acting through the processes of nature—has bestowed upon the human form.

COUNSELING SELF TO BALANCE
AND PREVENTING IMBALANCE

In the perspective of commitment to inner change, conscience, the highest form of perception, has been given two abilities to combat the negative experiences of the nurturing process: inherent attraction to what is right (*amr bil maruf*) in terms of inner balance and inherent rejection of what is wrong (*nahy an al-munkar*) or imbalance. When the nurturing process reinforces these two self—regulating abilities, the return to the spirit within, although difficult, does not require tremendous discipline as the self has already been educated little by little over time through a nurturing system that enhances the nature originated by God. Without a balanced nurturing process, the return is possible but requires an even greater struggle. From the stories related below, it becomes clear that seven Sufi women had very different nurturing environments yet each in her own way was able to effect the return to her God-given nature and attain balance through commitment to inner change.

PROFILES OF SUFI WOMEN OF AMERICA

Let us first get a picture of each of these seven women. Four of them will tell the story of their conversion to Islam and then their decision to take initiation in the Naqshbandi order.[21] One of the seven submitted to God's Will and made the commitment to inner change at the same time. Of the two who were born Muslim, one was also born Naqshbandi.

Two are Euro-American, Hoda and Latifa. Three are Afro-American: Aliya, Khadija and Rasheedah. Two are emigrants: Bagha from Iran and Hajja Nazihc from Syria. All of them are in their 40s. Hoda is a poet. Latifa teaches Islamic Art and Architecture at the University of Victoria. Aliya is a social worker who also taught in her local Islamic Sunday school for many years. Khadija is a teacher who taught in Dar al-Islam in Abiquiu and now teaches in Michigan. Rasheedah is also a working mother with a degree in psychology and certification as a hypnotherapist. Five were single mothers at the time of their submission to God's will. Bagha is a businesswoman. Hajja Nazihe is the daughter of Shaykh Nazim who represents five different Sufi orders including the Naqshbandi order of which he is the current international leader. Hajja Nazihe is also the wife of Shaykh Hisham Kabbani, Shaykh Nazim's representative in North America.

Part II: Awakening

CHAPTER 1: ACCEPTING SUBMISSION TO GOD'S WILL

INTRODUCTION

For four of the women—Latifa, Aliya, Rasheedah and Khadija—their awakening began by recovering the knowledge which had somehow always been with them—belief in the oneness of God. This long held belief was put into action when they consciously submitted to God's Will. Each tells a different story, but underlying each story is the innate belief in the oneness of God.

SUFI WOMEN

LATIFA

I live in British Columbia and have been Muslim for fourteen years. I was brought up as a Catholic. I was the kind of kid who was always bothering my parents to go to church. I was interested in charismatic Catholicism as a teenager and then in my early twenties I began to be disillusioned. I could not reconcile myself with the concept of the trinity and the idea that Jesus, peace be upon him, was the son of God. I became a lapsed Catholic.

Then when I was twenty-six I met some Muslims who were from Trinidad who had themselves converted having met some Ansar Allahs in Montreal and then some Sunni Muslims.

I was fascinated by them. I was always interested in people who made up the third world. We used to spend a lot of time talking and I asked a lot of questions. I began to read the Quran and realized that what they in fact were believing and practicing was what I fundamentally knew to be reality as a child: that there was One God.

The practices themselves of the Muslims were often colored by their cultures. It was very challenging to differentiate between what was Islam and what was someone's culture. It was challenging and at times it seemed to be insurmountable.

I was originally married to a Canadian who was not Muslim. Eventually his lack of belief in God and depression made it impossible to continue the relationship.

I then married a man from Eriteria simply because he was Muslim. I did not have access to Muslim men. We had a six and a half year marriage. Two children were the result of that marriage. Cultural differences, family problems and a battering relationship, as well, resulted in divorce.

ALIYA

I find it very difficult to speak about myself and my experiences as a Muslim convert but I will do my best for the faith of Islam to explain how Islam has reached the Afro-American community with the hope that it might spread to everyone here in North America.

Like many in this country, particularly Afro-Americans, I was raised as a Christian in a Christian family with pseudo-Christian beliefs. My father was an AME Christian minister with a Doctorate in Theology who pastored numerous churches in the south. He was an excellent speaker who could "move" people with his vivid stories of the Prophets and their trials. We moved constantly, about every two years, when I was growing up, from church to church in Georgia, Florida, Arkansas, and finally, North Carolina. More importantly for me, he and my mother had great faith in the One, Great, Almighty God. For over fifty years of ministry, he never wavered throughout his years of preaching and teaching. Finally, he was led to be a spokesman for the Civil Rights struggle, simple because he believed in a Just God which gave him and others courage to stand up against the "powers that be." As he put it, 'He was a drum major for justice!' I can never express the depth of my gratitude for this living example of love of God, faith, integrity and commitment. They gave all of their children that seed of faith that still guides me. Unfortunately, at a fairly young age, I discovered there was not enough basic practical information in my Christian belief to answer my questions. I discovered that there was not enough basic practical information coming from the religion or religious belief which was sufficient to answer the questions of maturity, the questions of growing up in the repressive system of segregation and racism in this country. I found that Christianity did not offer enough practicality to direct my life. I was very confused after having been given such an upbringing.

I cannot recall exactly my first experience with Islam. I believe it was when I was studying in the university in Europe, living out of the United States in the university setting in Oxford, England. There I met Muslims from Nigeria who had apparently a very rich history of Islam besides experience of religious knowledge in the particular language of Arabic and Hausa.

Unfortunately I was not taught the basic tenets of Islam other than what I could learn from association. I was impressed with the integrity of the people, of the life and joy of the people and also with their sense of love. There was no hint of inferiority which I had experienced among the Afro-Americans who had grown up in the West. There was no hint of resentment *per se* although these were people who were suffering from the throes of colonialism, neo-colonialism and, consequently, racism.

I felt that these were people who had a genuine love for all people. They had a very keen religious sense, a moral sense of right and wrong and as I said a strong sense of love and unity for all people. These people were also politically astute. They did not like the English colonialists who had come to their country and their continent and had done such devastating things in terms of the economy, the religious life, the social life. They had carved up whole areas of territory, pitted people against people, tribal group against tribal group. While they had experienced this and expressed their distress with the English colonial system and the neo-colonialists who were now descending on their new nations, there was still an underlying appreciation for the humanity of everyone which I greatly admired.

This was my first real experience and taste of Islam, through observing the character of these people, observing how these Africans, these Hausa, lived including some of the Nigerians who were not Muslim. I could not understand the racial grouping of this community which ran across color lines. The Nigerians could communicate perfectly with the Muslims of Egypt, the Persians, the Muslims of Arabia. There was a community there which I had never felt among people before as strongly as I felt among these Muslims. There were also Ethiopians there as well. It was just the sense that, 'I know you. You are my sister. You are my brother.'

It was through this experience that I tasted Islam although I had very little knowledge of it. I did not even know enough to ask intelligent questions. Unfortunately they did not feel compelled to tell me too much because they felt I was already Muslim even though I had explained to them that I was not and that I had come from a Christian background. I was ignorant about religion. I did not know what to ask and how to ask it.

It was many years later after returning to the US in the late 60s and early 70s that I observed Islam in this country among Afro-Americans in the form of the Nation of Islam among Afro-Americans, who at that time were the most visible group both politically and religiously, the most viable. They had the most life, the most direction. They were also the most outspoken and the most visible. They had a power of attraction among our people which I did not understand. Frankly I did not experience it first hand but I did see the evidence of their practice in the communities, community life, their ability to attract Afro-American people and to transform their lives from alcoholism and prostitution into energetic, vital, moral lives. There was a concentration on family. There was concentration on economic development which would have newly resurrected points in our community, open in the 60s after the passage of the public accommodation laws and others which improved the lives of this community. On the other hand, I was acutely aware that what I was observing in the Nation of Islam was not entirely religious expression. Their leaders had distorted religious belief with a mythology of nationalism which did not embody absolute Truth. Religious belief does not discriminate. It is color blind. Neither is it based on imagination. I could never accept. I could not become a convert.

That was my second experience. But again, because I was not experiencing it first hand, I did not have the taste, the feel. I just observed it. I admired the people whom I saw who identified themselves as Muslims.

Of course I admired Malcolm, al-Hajj Malik al-Shabbaz, as everyone did. We all loved Malcolm. We did not know how to describe it and why but we knew that there was some power there, some force, some force of commitment, intelligence, spirituality that was both admired and feared. He had an awesome appeal to the Afro-American. He opened up an international structure that I first felt in Europe but which I could not articulate to anyone else. I had seen pure Africans as citizens of the world. They could negotiate, talk to, be friends of, be teachers of anybody and there was not that sense of inferiority which I had experienced as an Afro-American in this country.

It was years later—after I had matured, had a family life, divorced, worked when I finally returned to North Carolina to my parents' home place—that I had my final initiation. I say initiation because in the other two were encounters I never accepted the religion of Islam. The third time that it happened was much more powerful and I could not refuse. It was approximately ten years ago, perhaps more. After completing one year of law school in one of the southern universities, I did not enjoy university life at all. I did not enjoy the first year of law school at all as most students would attest but something happened after that experience which I cannot express adequately.

I had a burning desire, a compulsion to begin to learn about Islam. I had been asking God in a general way or through meditation and prayer. I was asking to be directed, to be guided. Out of nowhere I felt compelled to find out more, to seek knowledge about Islam. I remember going through the telephone directory for the addresses of local mosques. I found one. I called. It happened to be a Friday just before the Friday congregational prayer. I spoke to someone there and asked if it were possible just to come and visit the mosque. The person said, 'Yes please come. In fact we have gotten to the point in our city where we are combining all of the various mosque Friday services into one service here, and one of the local prayer leaders is giving the sermon for everyone, so you are welcome to come.'

I remember asking at the end, 'Is this the Nation of Islam or is this really Islam?'

The person went silent but he was very tactful. He said, 'I think they are from the Nation here but there are also others of other persuasions, Sunni Muslims, so please come and discover for yourself.'

I did go to my first Friday congregational prayer in North Carolina. I remember hearing the call to prayer where I was actually sitting in a group of Muslims. I remember sensing that this was the most ancient sound that I had ever heard. I could feel the hair stand up on the back of my neck when I heard this and I knew at that moment that this was what I had been looking for. There was a tremendous sense of joy.

I don't remember what the sermon was about, but afterwards I remember speaking to the sisters for a very long time. Someone gave me a book to read, *Islam in Focus*. They invited me back. I was very impressed with the warmth of the people, the sincerity, the light coming from the people. I remember speaking to someone who had been living in California when I was out there a few years prior to this who invited me to come by and attend another prescribed prayer and a sister's class. Again I don't think anyone expected this, but I took the invitation seriously and followed up on it the following Sunday.

There was one sister there who told me about a particular community and mosque. She invited me to come to other events and classes. The next time that I went I took my daughter who was at that time about eight years old. She followed me. I immediately started taking classes. The first class happened to be a children's weekend school. It was more for my daughter than for myself but I would go and act as the cafeteria help. I used to serve the lunch and at the same time read everything I could find. It was a small Sunni community. The prayer leader of the community was a person who had been delegated to do the sermon for the city to bring all the Muslims together. It was fortunate from that standpoint. It is a community that had been developed from the Islamic party of North America. Their prayer leader was one who had been raised Islamically on the diet of Islam out of Washington DC. There was a strong emphasis on reading and knowledge in this community and learning aspects of the Divine Law. As I look back on it was a fortunate experience from that standpoint because I did get a lot of basic reading in Islam.

The other experience which capped this in cement for me was that at the same time that I was seeking to find Islam, I took the chance of writing to a person I had met twenty years before. I sent a letter. I went to the local library and researched addresses and that kind of thing. Sure enough it made its mark and returned from this student friend of mine who wrote and congratulated me on accepting Islam but said, 'I thought you were always Muslim.' The person sent me a book, *Towards Understanding Islam*.

So the acceptance of Islam not only came from my heart searching for the truth for God, but it was also accompanied by some reading and knowledge. I was invited both ways. Praise be to God, it was enough to seal it. I can remember having a Quran of my own for the first time, reading the Opening Chapter and going down in prostration because I knew that this was the truth. I cried all the way through. I read the Quran cover to cover in English. I read the commentary. I read every line of commentary. This was so exciting for me because I knew for the first time that I had found something that was real and permanent—truth—and would not fade or diminish with time.

I was so grateful. I had one long distance phone call with the person who was gracious enough to send me the book and reinforce my effort to turn towards Islam. I never saw this person again but praise belongs to God, it was enough encouragement in the form of a letter to get me really started.

I started offering the prescribed prayers before I had really learned them. I made the transition to the modest dress very quickly because it was almost as if I were being instructed every step of the way and I could not resist the instruction this time. I began wearing the modest dress which caused great resentment from my father and mother because at that time my daughter and I were living with them. There was a tremendous struggle. The resentment and anger at my becoming Muslim almost became unbearable, but I knew this was a course I had to take. I knew it was one that would make me happy.

It was an experience I could share with my daughter. She could grow to be Muslim and I was extremely happy. She was at the critical stage of pre-adolescence when she was experiencing a strong sense of self-expression and was becoming painfully aware of "peer-pressure." She wanted so much to fit in and be accepted that it made her hesitate slightly. I tried not to force Islam on her ["There is no compulsion in religion"], but I did urge her little by little to pray and to cover her hair. She was so bright and good. Her heart was immediately open to praying as Muslims pray, but balked at dressing differently. Finally, she came to me one day and announced she was resigning from her ballet classes at the School of the Arts as this no longer appealed to her. Quietly her heart was being illumined and her sense of modesty was reflected without my coercion in the choices she made in her clothing and activities.

This is the road. This is the path. She struggled with it and loved the relationships she was developing with some of the other young Muslims. It was not however without difficulty. Some of the expectations she had of perfect friendship and perfect relationship did not work. Their parents had just learned Islam a half a generation ago so they were struggling with their own adjustment. However much of the time it was very joyful.

I don't know how I was able to resist the resentment coming from my father, living in his house, but somehow God gave me the strength to hold on and not to give up. We were able to keep our prescribed prayers, our fast and we were able to wear our modest dress daily. By God's mercy and as I learned later by the blessings of our shaykh who had been holding us all this time, I was able to earn a professional living, wearing the full modest dress. Praise belongs to God, the more steadfast we became, the more doors were open for us even with the difficulties my daughter was having adjusting.

Her sense of peer pressure was much more than mine. She experienced some ridicule from the kids at school. They poked fun at her. I kept telling her—this was junior high—to be a good Muslim and God willing in time she will be able to see the fruit of what God has enabled her to do. Sure enough as she matured into high school, I could see it happening. The young people began to look up to her instead of calling her names. They were seeking her out for advice. The tables turned with God's mercy. It was not overnight but it was a gradual profound turn. As the people in the community began to look at us with respect, praise belongs to God, with God's blessings, we were able to carry the weight of all of this.

This experience is not too different from many Muslims who convert to Islam. I think that among Afro-American it might not be as hard a transition as among other groups. I don't know. The Afro-American people have Islam in their hearts. It is clear. We have it on our tongues as we struggle to pronounce the Arabic which we have forgotten, but with which perhaps we came as slaves. This was the culture that was stripped from us, along with the language and religion. Most critically, the religion of Islam was taken from us through slavery.

There have been many documented accounts of slaves who came to the West, north or central or south America. They were indeed Muslims who brought the Arabic language and Islam with them along with their indigenous languages. This was lost as a result of slavery which tore families apart, which forbade reading and writing even if it was in another language which we did not understand. They separated children from parents. They forbade the dress of the African people. They systematically broke them over time, a period which lasted over four hundred years. We lost the outward expression of the religion, but we maintained the inner secrets of the heart. As Afro-Americans we have retained those secrets which were put into our hearts which gave us knowledge of the religion, knowledge of the prophets, and spiritual knowledge, knowledge that I think was hidden knowledge is still retained within us as a people no matter how debased we have become as a result of the life here in the West.

I think it has helped the emigrant Muslims to stand up—those who want to hide their Islam, by giving courage to those afraid of the West, afraid of the not fitting in—and more than anything wanting to fit into the material life here. It helps them stand proud perhaps because people like Malcolm, people like the honorable Elijah Muhammad, were not afraid to share their religious and political beliefs with the people of this country. Leaders like them held the hope that they could bring about a moral understanding of Reality to the people here who are so much in darkness as a result of the tyranny of democracy, of racism, of oppression, of color consciousness and of materialism. That experience cannot be underrated. In my own life it was probably that plus the other two personal experiences which brought Islam as a reality to me, my family, and my daughter.

After that time I lived in North Carolina as a Sunni Muslim for almost ten years, working in the mosque again as a single person. It was very difficult as a single woman wanting to do what I could. I participated in conferences. I taught the sisters' class. This was how time passed along with meeting family, work responsibilities and the responsibility of raising my daughter.

KHADIJA

I remember seeking truth and spiritual leadership at a very young age, nine perhaps. I grew up with a grandfather who was a Methodist minister with a small store front congregation in Harlem. I sang the lovely gospel numbers and constantly asked questions my grandfather couldn't answer. They irritated him so I lost interest in his church and sought elsewhere. I looked for truth in the Catholic church. For months I went to mass with my friends. In eighth grade I took Latin so I could read the original Vulgate Bible, I hoped. After that was my Baptist phase. Still no answers, no real fulfillment outside the music. I went to Reverend Ike with my paternal grandmother. He was one of those TV type evangelist pretty boys taking in those weekly donations that kept up his grand hall and cadillacs and his wife in furs.

I remember walking through Harlem one day and hearing one of the Nation of Islam's ministers, maybe even Malcolm X. I stopped to listen for a while, went home and looked up Islam in the encyclopedia. I was looking for Elijah Muhammad but found instead Prophet Muhammad. Even with their misinformation about "Muhammadanism" and some of the strange practices they attributed to its followers, I was touched.

The account of the cave and the first revelation brought tears to my eyes at twelve. I fell in love with Prophet Muhammad and gave up Jesus from that tainted article in the *World Book Encyclopedia*. It took five more years for me to walk into Temple No. 7 and receive my X as "soldier" under

Minister Louis Farrakhan as a faithful Muslim Girl in Training (M.G.T.. Those were the only Muslims I could find as Sunni Muslims were not actively doing propagation as the brothers and sisters in the Nation of Islam were doing. I knew I needed leadership and I could feel Islam was right, but somehow this was not the religion I fell in love with as an adolescent.

The Nation held many things that I craved—economic independence for African-Americans, respect and dignity for black women, protection and social belonging, but something wasn't right. Only God knows why I needed to spend those years with that organization before finally moving on to the Sunnah (Traditions) of Prophet Muhammad whom I was seeking all along.

RASHEEDAH

I feel perhaps a little additional background is needed to explain how and why I came to Islam. I prefer to say that I reverted since the Quran tells us that all human beings are born Muslim and that it is their parents that make them into something else.

When I was about seven years old I was looking at a TV program that featured Muslims praying. I heard the call to prescribed prayer. I was absolutely fascinated.

It touched something deep inside of me. I asked my father, who happened to be in the room at the time, what they were doing. He explained that they were 'Moslems', as he called them, and that they were praying.

I told him at that time, 'We'll that's what I am.'

He said, 'OK.' He humored me with what he thought were whims, knowing that I was searching as all human beings are even at a young age, for my niche in life.

I would say that my becoming Muslim later was not surprising at all. I had always been interested in comparative religion. I loved long dresses and scarves. I thought they were absolutely beautiful. This is from childhood.

My grandfather on my mother's side was a Baptist minister. He was a very, very God loving man and he encouraged my love for God. He realized early on that there were some things in Christianity with which I was not comfortable. He explained these things to me in an historical perspective in such a way that I understood that the things that made me uncomfortable were not things that were part of the teachings of Jesus Christ, upon whom be peace. They were things that were brought into the religion after the events of the crucifixion either by Paul (formerly Saul of Tarsus), by the Council of Nicea or the result of interpolations and mis-translations. So while he probably would have wanted me to be Christian, he certainly understood when at the age of seventeen it was my decision that I did not want to be Christian and that I in fact wanted to be Muslim.

He knew something about Islam because they study comparative religions to some extent in the Baptist Seminary from which he graduated. Since he did have a Doctorate of Divinity, he probably knew quite a bit more about comparative religion than he actually discussed with me preferring to let me learn these things for myself. Islam is a complete way of life, not a persona that we adopt on Fridays, or at a mosque or other Islamic gathering. Islam gives believers a very unique world view and frame of reference. There is no superiority based upon race, color, nationality, sex or any other external attribute. Muslims world-wide are one Community bound to one another by their love for God and his last Messenger, Muhammad Ibn Abdullah (ﷺ). When I was eighteen years old, I made the declaration of faith saying, 'There is no god but God and Muhammad is the Messenger of God,' with the Ahmadiyyat movement in Islam. This was in 1968.

I came to Ahmadiyyat purely by accident. I looked in the yellow pages under religious organizations. I called several that were listed there and the only really warm and positive response that I got was from an Ahmadiyya missionary. I went to his office. He gave me books and taught me Islam. Once I had a pretty firm foundation in the basic tenets of Islam, I began to hear certain allusions to Mirza Ghulam Ahmad as the promised messiah and mahdi, concepts with which, in light of my studies, I was not really comfortable. In the course of time I eventually drifted away from the Ahmadiyyat movement altogether.

I joined MSA and went to mosques all over the city. I did not play an active role in another Islamic community until I joined Jamaat al-Muslimeen and the Islamic Party of North America in 1972. The prayer leader of that community was a brother who is now my husband of five years, Dawud Salahuddin. Both Jamaat al-Muslimeen and the Islamic Party played major roles in my religious and spiritual development.

Dawud stressed "common sense Islam." He stressed "the spirit of the law" and understanding of the spirit of the law so that one can better understand "the letter of the law." This has always been my philosophy of life. If a thing does not make sense to me, it is quite difficult for me to adhere to it. If I don't understand why and how it fits into the overall scheme of things, I cannot relate to it in any meaningful way.

Both Jammat al-Muslimeen and the Islamic Party stressed scholarship as did Prophet Muhammad (ﷺ). Since the acquisition of knowledge is incumbent upon every Muslim "from the cradle to the grave," we were eager to acquire it. We were encouraged to learn from the scholars by reading what they had written, discussing it with one another and attempting to apply what we had learned to our daily lives. We acquired knowledge, not for show, but because knowledge and wisdom are the building blocks of inner change. There is a reliable Tradition which states that the greatest danger to Islam in the latter days would be the preponderance of ignorant followers. I seek refuge in my Lord from both ignorance and arrogance.

Chapter 2: Committing Self to Inner Change

Introduction

Six of the seven women made a conscious commitment to inner change, while one was born into it. Fortified with the knowledge of God's oneness and their commitment to it, the women realized that acceptance of submission to God's Will (*islam*) was still not effecting a profound inner change. They related better to others than they had previously, but they still questioned some of their actions. They sensed outer change but then realized without inner growth, the outer was but a partial change. Six of them, then, took initiation in a Sufi order. This was done with the hope that initiation would be the key to unlocking their inner states and that with this commitment, each would be able to change by transforming persistent negative traits into positive ones.

We begin with the story of the one woman who was born into both submission to God's Will and commitment to inner change, Hajji Nazihe. Also we will meet Hoda and Bagha here for the first time. Hoda both submitted to God's Will and made a commitment to inner change at the same time while Bagha was born into the faith of submission to God's Will, and later in life, made a commitment to inner change. Following that, Latifa, Aliya, Khadija and Rasheedah express how they resolved their commitment to inner change.

SUFI WOMEN

HAJJA NAZIHE

I was born in a family whose father's side traces its lineage back to Sayyid Abd al-Qadir Jilani and whose mother's side traces its lineage back to Jalal al-Din Rumi. My mother was born in Russia in the area of Kazan and they followed the Naqshbandi Sufi Way in Chechnia and other areas. The Naqshbandi Sufi order was flourishing at the time of the Tsar and before that in the Russian area. There were many Naqshbandis there.

At the time of the communist revolution, my maternal grandfather, who was very wealthy, felt the threat against Sufism and against Islam. He decided to leave that area of Kazan and to migrate to a safer place like the Middle East and Turkey.

My mother's family suffered a great deal in the migration from Russia to Turkey. My grandfather took whatever he could of his money in gold coins for the trip. He wanted to hide the gold in a cave but as he was going there he had to cross a river. The gold fell into the river and he lost everything. He decided that for the sake of Islam he must keep moving. They ate grass, leaves and fruit from the trees until they reached Turkey. They lived there for twelve years where my maternal grandfather settled until the time of time of the last Ottoman Emperor, Sultan Abd al-Hamid. When Mustafa Kamal came, he forbid the practice of religion. My family then fled from Turkey to Syria where they settled and where I was born.

My maternal grandfather knew that Damascus was a city of Sufis, a city where Sufism was practiced. He looked for a Naqshbandi Sufi shaykh and met Grandshaykh Abd Allah al-Daghestani. He helped him build his mosque and the first Sufi center of Damascus for people from Daghestan and Chechnia, people coming from Russia. At the same time, Maulana

Shaykh Nazim came from Istanbul, Turkey to meet with Grandshaykh. He met my mother there in Damascus and they were married with the blessings of Grandshaykh who said that it was a blessed marriage. Praise belongs to God, it was a good match because they had opened their hearts to each other. This is what is written on the Preserved Tablet—she is your wife for the rest of your life. They married and my mother lived in the house of Grandshaykh for one year. She learned all the ethics, good manners, how to serve, how to teach and knowledge of Sufism. Grandshaykh gave her permission to spread that knowledge to women.

I was born after two years of their marriage and was raised in my mother and father's home, but more often in Grandshaykh's home. I considered him to be my grandfather. I loved him more than I loved my uncles and relations, cousins, etc. Whenever my mother went looking for me, she would find me in Grandshaykh's house. Our homes were very near to one another so that I grew up in a very intellectual Sufi family. I was raised in a community in that area where great scholars used to come to listen to Grandshaykh and Maulana Shaykh Nazim. Intellectual women scholars used to come to my mother and listen to her. My childhood, then, was always listening to healing, debates, lectures on Sufism and on the Divine Law.

HODA

While studying in Europe, trips to Morocco and Turkey increased my interest in Islamic art and architecture. I then began reading widely in Islam and in Sufism to enhance my understanding and appreciation of Islamic culture. Although Sufism intrigued me and seemed to comport well with the traditions of other religions with which I was familiar, I found certain practices of Islam offensive to my western sensibilities. As both my interest in Sufism and my time spent in the Middle East increased, I elected to convert partly as an expedient to learn more about Sufism. Although I now took Islam more seriously, I still considered myself an ardent admirer of

Buddhism and of Central Asian Shamanism not to mention my muted residual interest in Christianity which factored further into the mix. This situation obtained until a singularly fortuitous event occurred. I met Shaykh Nazim al-Haqqani in Damascus, Syria, in 1978 at which point Islamic Sufism ceased to be a spectator sport. I began to eat the food instead of the menu.

For me commitment to inner change is the heart of submission to God's Will, the very heart of life itself here and hereafter. What it means in my daily life boils down to some very simple goals mainly just to be, to be sincerely in my right spot, to be this little sand grain in simple harmony with the great wheeling pattern whose light I barely register. In other words I want to sit down and pay attention. I want to untie the knot of separation. May God help me and forgive me.

BAGHA

This is the first time I have put my thoughts together about the impact of Sufism on my life. I have always considered Sufism to be the *raison d'etre* of my life. It is as indispensable to my soul as breath is to my body. It is my Lord's gift to me just as my heart and eyes are. I was initiated on the Day of the Allocation of Recourses by the only Fair Judge. He provided me with the method and technique of maintaining my allegiance and confirming God as my only Lord. Therefore, I have never been separate from Sufism and never devoid of the remembrance of God even before I was born.

I was born after my parents lost their first sweet and beloved daughter. Burning with the desire to have another daughter, my mother tells me that one night she had a dream. Next day the prayer leader of the mosque was interpreting the dream to my father. He said, 'You and your wife are blessed by the Prophet's family. You will have a baby girl who will serve the cause of the Prophet.'

A few months later my mother was pregnant. My father was a military pilot. I was just born when my father's name appeared on the list of martyrs of the war. Later he was found but there was talk that his leg would have to be amputated. After a long recovery, he was sent back home on his own legs! This was miraculous, the Bestowers' gift, the arrival of the father and the baby celebrated at once.

They say I was calm and solitary. My main childhood memory is my intimate relationship with an antelope. Although imaginary, it was more real, lively and understanding than anyone. It was between shadow and matter. We were soul mates in perfect harmony and accord. It would pick me up on its back and fly in the sky where there were no one and no worries. Our freedom was a conscious freedom. We became clairvoyant. We could help out the needy and stop the mischievous. Our oneness in decisions and actions was natural and instantaneous. I did not know or ask where and how it appeared. I lost its physical trace when I was twelve or thirteen. However, I feel it present in my heart always.

I loved to stay home alone and read. I found myself reading two or three books at the same time. Dante's three trips to the lands of purgatory, heaven and hell expressed in powerful words and magnificent drawings impressed me at nine. The book of hell was scary and the most strange and interesting. The book of heaven was extremely uplifting and my first encounter with the intellect (*aql*) and love (*ishq*) dilemma. Dante's very respectable teacher, Virgil, could only take him up to a certain sky whereas his dream mistress Beatrice, gracefully and easily took him to the highest heaven.

My antelope friend and books plunged me more into my inner world which was perfect and natural. However, it was painful, but indispensable not to look bizarre in society. It was hard to blend with the outside world. Coping with shyness, isolation and simplicity, used to drain my energy. Being physically stronger than most boys of my age, I did not like playing with girls and dolls. Boys were like fire that could be approached only up to a point. It took me three decades to blend in. I became hardworking outside and meditative inside. I only discovered recently that in order to cope with our biggest problem which is separation from God, each one adopts a different life style according to one's nature and nurture.

At about the age of twenty I came to know that most of the time our desire for physical pleasures is stronger than the pleasure itself. The pleasures of the mind are greater than the pleasures of the world. Later when we taste spiritual joy, all worldly pleasures become nonsense and are bleached out.

I had done post graduate and doctoral studies in child education at the Sorbonne and Harvard and opened a day care center in Tehran when three years later came the surprise of the Iraq-Iran war. Day and night rockets were hitting buildings. It was a test for everyone to bear never knowing if the next bomb would hit them. My nursery day care consisted of 150 students. Critical issues like children's safety, nutrition, physical and psychological well-being demanded my attention and hard work during the war. At times the job seemed overwhelming and out of control because the essential was missing. I yielded to a desperate need for someone who could help me with all of my personal and social responsibilities. Day and night, the march of work and the serenade of prayer were going on until my yoga master introduced me to a shaykh who had just begun his Sufi teachings. His name is Shaykh Paikan Shaibani. After a few sessions I found his approach to Sufism was interesting and related to practical life. He was super-intelligent, determined and funny.

His first objective was to unfold the reality of Islam for us. His students were mainly western-oriented new age people in search of truth. Being an architect-engineer, the shaykh was trying to relate exoteric Islam and jurisprudence to science and modern belief system in order to relate better to the new age group.

On the esoteric side, he confined himself to the remembrance of God (*dhikr*) which he said is the most powerful tactic for emergency conditions like the ones we faced. He told us to do our spiritual practice of remembrance of God twice a day, twenty minutes in the morning and at night as beginners.

Within a month we could observe how our walking, hand-

Committing Self to Inner Change 43

writing, eating and sleeping habits and even our tone of voice changed as the shaykh had told us. Our patience and ability to cope with daily matters increased in some fields and decreased in others. Our interests and dislikes started to evolve. We could not wait until the day for our group remembrance of God liturgy came.

Meetings took place twice a week. He started with ten people. In a year at least three hundred people were attending his meetings and the capable ones covered the whole Quran in one to three hours of recitation.

He picked a group of about twenty people for the most intense schedule the next Ramadan. For forty nights we recited the Quran's 114 chapters in a special order instead of sleeping and went to work after the dawn prescribed prayer.

Sometimes he took us hiking. We gathered together before dawn at the foot of the mountain. Walking in the dark on a narrow path above the valley, we could only see one step ahead. This kept us concentrating constantly on the path. We could not be in the future or the past because of the fragility and importance of the present.

It is clear that our state of consciousness definitely shifted during the hiking project. For instance, at times one of us might become so tired and exhausted that he was sure his fall was imminent. But what could one do? There was no choice but to keep going. The shaykh and the group continued their climb. One could not stay alone in the mountain and get lost or eaten by animals. So he or she tried to reach the next camping station in the mountain. Once there, looking down and seeing the narrow path which had taken us up, we forget about the hardship of the path. Having lived with our mind's tricks and our true power, we tasted the joy of our performance. In this way we were getting lessons in patience, endurance, mindfulness and mindlessness. The group performed remembrance of God exercises on the mountain on the way up or down. Afterward, the shaykh said the mountain had represented our animal being which we had to surmount.

He instructed us to relate to our guardian angel. He then

asked us to write a paper on our guardian angel and communicate with it. At this point we found out how weak we were. He gave us each one Quranic word on which to write a paper. I remember mine was "darriah." He collected the papers, but we only knew later that the paper should be written for and collected by our heart.

The shaykh repeatedly told us that if we had a watermelon in our hands, we had to be ready at any time to put it down to pick up a bag of gold. One day he told us that his responsibility towards us had ended and that we had to go and practice what the Quran had taught us, along with our invocations, in our every day life. It was depressing and sickening. I was confused again like the day before meeting the shaykh. Later I knew that he had an undeniable unique and immense effect on my life. It would be impossible to thank him for what he did for us.

Not appreciating what the shaykh had put in my hand, I traveled here to America to join my family. Although I adopted a new life style, Sufism did not lose its meaning for me. I read more Sufi books. Upon the invitation of a friend, I attended meetings of the Bawa Muhaiyaddeen Fellowship in Boston, Massachusetts. Although I knew about Bawa right after he passed away, his sincerity and perfect purity and extraordinary physical life attracted me immediately. He had said that a lot of his followers had not yet joined him or even been born. He expressed the knowledge of highest sphere of consciousness in simple practical words and breath taking songs. Love, compassion and wisdom poured forth from his humble, powerful and impeccable manners. He answered my questions and solved my problems quickly in the most personal way. He is super vigilant on all his disciples and supports and heals them in difficult times. Every time I visited his shrine and mosque in Philadelphia, he would load my heart with his unique lessons. The last time I went to the shrine, I was in Philadelphia on my way back to Virginia. To my absolute surprise, Bawa gave me neither lessons nor a hint of communication.

While I was in Philadelphia, I met Shaykh Hisham Kabbani. He was talking in a relaxed and friendly way to his audience. I thought the fact that Bawa had for the first time not communicated to my heart was his way of introducing me to a new Sufi order's teachings as well. I joined the Naqshbandi order and benefitted a lot.

Latifa

It was not until I left my second husband that I strongly felt the need for spirituality and discovered Islamic spirituality that I had read about in books. Despite the fact that I was an academic, I had not realized that Sufism was still existent. I assumed as I had been told that Sufism was something that belonged in the Middle Ages, that it decayed very quickly, that it was dead. I was delighted to find out two and one half years ago that this was far from the truth. I think it had something to do with leaving my marriage which helped me feel free to do that. I had felt very restricted.

My husband's belief in Islam was, in fact, an extremely restrictive view, very oppressive. I felt chafed under it. I finally came to the conclusion that his religion and my religion did not seem to be the same religion at all. I either had to leave my religion or to leave him and I chose to leave him.

About six months after I did so I was at an academic conference and almost unconsciously I expressed interest in Sufism. The person I was speaking with was a disciple of Shaykh Nazim who gave me Shaykh Hisham's telephone number. About three weeks after that I phoned him. I took initiation with him discovering that Sufism, the science of inner knowledge, is alive and well within Islam. So I have been trying to follow the shaykh since then.

The biggest blessing that I have learned since being initiated into a group oriented toward commitment to inner change is that the purpose of our work here, the goal of it, is to suppress our egos, to tame our egos and to self-efface.

ALIYA

After this period of time there were two people who came to our mosque in Winston-Salem. They were a husband and wife from Cyprus. I was genuinely impressed with their warmth, with their sense of love, their lack of racism. So often people who would come to this particular Afro-American mosque were a little bit condescending to us. They felt they had to come and help the poor Afro-American learn Islam. Praise belongs to God, we accepted them because we knew there were so many things that we did not know and did not pretend to know like the language. But so often those who brought that knowledge were so condescending and so arrogant that it made the people resentful and we did not get much accomplished.

These people were different. Apparently they saw something different in my daughter and myself. They invited us to their home. When we entered their home we saw that they had a photo of some religious leader with very piercing blue eyes who was leading the remembrance of God service, something I had not heard before, the recitation of God's names and praising God.

I had never heard this before. In my mosque I was told that this was innovation. We felt that others might say this about us. We have never experienced first hand remembrance of God liturgy. I was later told by this remarkable couple that the photograph was that of Maulana Shaykh Nazim al-Qubrusi of Cyprus, Turkey and that he was leading the remembrance of God liturgy in London. They showed us a video of Peckham, London. I was amazed. I had never heard anything like it. I had never heard remembrance of God like this. I had never seen anyone who was so captivating and so dignified and so compelling as Maulana Shaykh Nazim. I was so happy. I wanted to cry because it freed me from so many of the concepts that had been driven into me over the years. They brought the light and love that I felt when I first accepted this Islam. The lightness of spirit, the light, the purity of it, the power of it. It is as if it were coming back to me all again but in a way that was more articulate than the beginning had been. My heart was opening as I watched Shaykh Nazim. I was becoming happy again because I had been burdened down by the kind of dryness of Islam that I had been taught in this little community. I had become very disillusioned with communities or with the visible expression of Islam.

I felt honored to have been introduced to Shaykh Nazim through the presence of this couple. They told me many stories of people who had come from all over the world to meet him. It was apparent that it was not an ordinary person who I was watching. They gave me *Mercy Oceans* and talks of Abd Allah Daghestani. They showed me the mercy side of Islam which I had forgotten and had not seen demonstrated in the Islam I was practicing—God wants to see us enter Paradise, wants us to succeed in the tests of life. This was a new side I had not experienced before. It made me cry. There was so much goodness in what he was saying. I had never thought of good manners in God's presence, the giving of the traditional greetings, eating with the right hand. I wanted to learn more. This opened Sufism for me to meet two of his disciples who were living in a small town in North Carolina.

I wanted to see him in person, to sit in the association, to be participate in the remembrance of God liturgy that he led. This was the greatest thing I could do. I asked God in my heart to be able to go to visit. The great test was my daughter who was a freshman in Florida, many miles away. She had no idea who he was but in less than seven days she got her passport. We made it to London. So much life, so much elation. It was 1992. We were initiated on the first night. It was so unbelievable. The experience was overwhelming

Maulana Shaykh Nazim brings us to London each year to be tested because the streets are not an adequate place to test us. It is there in the confines of Peckham mosque in London. It is a test because it is overcrowded. It is cold. People are irritable. There are not enough showers. People from all over the world, from Europe, from Malaysia, from the US, from South America, all kinds of people, and they are all being watched by

Maulana Shaykh Nazim. We go there to be tested and to train our ego. He said that is why we go there. We are not going for comfort. We are going to be trained.

KHADIJA

I have been Muslim for twenty-four years. I am a Naqshbandi of Shaykh Nazim and Shaykh Hisham. I was living in New York. I was sent to work at Dar al-Islam, the Islamic school in Abiquiu New Mexico. I ended up there in 1984 with a new husband, new baby and three other children from my previous marriage. It was on the dirt road up to the masjid that I saw a sister smiling a smile of contentment that I never saw before in any other Muslim. She was in her birkenstoks, holding her prayer beads, walking along the dusty road with her face shining as if she possessed everything any human being ever wanted. And she did. Rahma Lutz and many of the other sisters I would meet later had everything they wanted in Sufism. I wanted what that sister had. I wanted that spiritual fulfillment that I still craved. I vowed I would meet her and find out what she had that I still did not have.

She was very gracious in sharing Shaykh Nazim with me. I started reading the *Mercy Ocean* books and attending the ladies remembrance of God liturgy sessions. My heart was touched by Shaykh Nazim's words like I had finally found home. It felt like the encyclopedia feeling. I felt chills sometimes at the words. I felt stirring in my heart that I had never felt before. It seemed that I had never even been one who submits to God's Will before that and yet I had been practicing Islam for fourteen years.

When you submit to the guidance of a shaykh, a true shaykh with divine connections, one who follows the Divine Law, your life begins to change. I have grown more as a human being in the last ten years than I had in all my years previously. You can not really live without advancing spiritually. You can walk for years in circles unless you have God's helpers shining the flashlight on the path. I was so far away from God even in my modest dress and with the twenty-two chapters of the Quran I could recite. My heart was so closed until I met my shaykh who made me look at myself.

The shaykh, and I am speaking about Shaykh Nazim, my grandshaykh and Shaykh Hisham who is here with the disciples in America, they know and see our hearts. If you say you want God and righteousness, they will lead you down that path with tests. My heart was full of envy, selfishness and pride. My ego was running my life. I had felt that I had accepted submission to God's Will outwardly in outer track, in dress, the headpieces, really adorned in modest attire but my heart was not clean. I would still backbite. I would still talk about people. Really it had not changed my heart.

Even though I cannot say that I have reached anywhere significant even now because I have so much further to go, still, since coming to Shaykh Nazim I have changed my attitude, changed my heart, become a calmer person. I used to be afraid of things. My faith was not as strong. I used to care about not having enough money and about material things. I used to think that if I do this or if my husband would only do that then everything would be okay. Now I know God does everything anyway and it is not even about what I do. Just believe and submit. What I learned I can do is trust in God and do good for others.

When my husband left me a single mother of six children, I was without money for some time. I would have panicked in that situation before Sufism. One day I had thirty-eight cents in my wallet and I was still smiling. I looked at my can of whatever, alone on the shelf, that one moldy lemon and submitted to the fact that God had never let us starve and that I was going to make something to eat that night. An hour later a sister came to my door with a hundred dollar check that she and her husband were thinking I could use. And there are tons of incidents like this in all Sufi lives.

What has given me the calm to accept all that is coming to me is the practice—the mentioning of God constantly, the soothing remembrance of God liturgy (*dhikr*) and daily spiritual practices (*wird*). That constant getting up every morning with those early morning prayers, that sincere asking to change inside for the better, brings you internal peace. Standing with my shaykh gives me the feeling of total protection. It is hard for me to explain but it is a spectacular feeling.

Having Shaykh Hisham is the greatest blessing for which one could hope. I cannot achieve the level of spirituality I so desire without he and his wife. I have had the privilege this summer of really getting to know and learn from Hajji Nazihe. She can bring tears to my eyes with the level of wisdom and power she possesses, yet is sweet and humble and utterly feminine.

You know she is a powerhouse! Sufism is a heart thing. You have to feel it. Your heart knows the truth when it hears it. My shaykh is teaching me how to get out of the way because I am nothing and let he who is the power and might carry me and provide me with all I have ever dreamed of having. It is scary sometimes to let go and completely trust in God.

I finally feel like I am in the right place. The sister I saw in New Mexico initiated me. I cannot say I shine like she shines, but at least I am walking alongside her to my Lord. Only now am I learning what submission to God's Will is with the help of my shaykh. Submission to God's Will is giving sincerely to others—really wanting for your brother or sister what you want for yourself. I've learned something so simple from the shaykh—if you want more, give more. It is our ego holding onto everything that keeps us back. When I give, I guess that my hands are then empty enough to receive and God is Beneficent and Merciful.

I am sorry to say that I have spent many years of my life not loving. I am beginning to understand what love is—clean, healthy, unconditional human love. I am beginning to feel love for people. I have begun to stop backbiting and judging. I have begun to know that there is another way besides mine to view a situation. I am beginning to e patient with people. I am learning to listen more. I am learning to care. We really are not acting like human beings in this world. We are without simple intelligence and manners. I know that God has sent us help through our shaykhs. I really am beginning to develop faith. I feel like such a baby.

Just so no one worries, I am now teaching Language Arts at Crescent Academy in Canton, Michigan. I moved here after spending a glorious summer at the Haqqani Center in Fenton, Michigan. I did not want to be too far from Shaykh Hisham and other Naqshbandis. Still unmarried, but feeling fulfilled though incomplete, I was able to finish a Masters in Training and Learning Technologies before leaving New Mexico. I am now seeking publication of Muslim children's stories. My oldest sons are in Harvard graduate school and the University of Florida. I live with four wonderful children ages 9-13, all claiming allegiance to Shaykh Nazim and Shaykh Hisham. I thank God for everything.

Rasheedah

At this time I also was coming in contact with many people who were Muslim who had other ideas. One brother in particular introduced me to Sufism. He was kind of an *avant garde* brother. He was not a member of any particular Sufi order and in fact probably embraced some of the ideas and teachings of various Sufi orders as well as the spiritual disciplines of other religions. Since I had always been interested as well in the esoteric aspects of religion, the metaphysical aspects, if you will, Sufism, of course, appealed to me.

As it happens, soon after bearing witness to the oneness of God and the prophethood of Muhammad (ﷺ), I began to have recurring dreams in which I was told to seek the Naqshbandi shaykhs in the black tents of Kedar. I had no idea what a Naqshbandi shaykh was or where the black tents of Kedar were located. Nobody that I asked had any idea either. If they did, they did not tell me. At some point, probably about three years after I submitted to God's Will, I met a brother who had traveled extensively in the Middle East, especially Arabia. He explained to me that the Naqshbandi shaykhs were in fact the leaders of a Sufi order and that they lived in and taught in black tents on the plains of Kedar in Arabia. Although grateful for an explanation, I was not convinced that I was meant to actually travel to Arabia to find the Naqshbandi shaykhs.

Every time I traveled to a new city, I opened the yellow pages under religious organizations to see if Naqshbandi order or organization of any kind was located in that city. I never ever found any reference to Naqshbandi.

After years and years of this search, I became so frustrated that I asked God Almighty if it was His will that I find the Naqshbandi shaykhs that He make the way for me to do so. I just kind of "let go and let God's Will take over." Although I thought about it often, I never heard any reference to the Naqshbandi order outside of the dreams and yet I knew that somehow I would find my Naqshbandi shaykh or he would find me.

About ten years ago, Abdur Rashid and Ayesha Matthews returned to Chicago after having spent five years living, working and studying in Egypt. I called to welcome them back and we renewed our friendship. In one conversation with sister Ayesha, I mentioned my recurring dream to her. There was a moment of silence. Then she said, 'Just a minute. Let me let you speak to my husband.'

She called brother Abdur Rashid to the phone. I recounted to him my dream and he told me that he was a member of the Naqshbandi order. During his travels in Egypt, he had met members of many Sufi orders, but the order which touched his heart and his soul was the Naqshbandi Sufi order. He said that he had been initiated by Maulana Shaykh Nazim. He told me that the Chicago disciples had remembrance of God gatherings on Saturday nights, and that the gatherings moved around from place to place. He told me that when next they had this gathering at his apartment, he would invite me to participate. He did so and I went. I watched a video of Maulana Shaykh Nazim's associations and I was very impressed with him, but I did not really do anything else about it for a number of years. All the time I was still in contact with Abdul Rashid and Ayesha and as a result, I was pretty much aware of the things that were going on with the Chicago branch.

After a while I felt that I was ready to at least investigate things more thoroughly. I made the commitment to start going to the Saturday night remembrance of God gathering. At that time the gatherings were still moving from place to place. My twin sons and I really enjoyed having something interesting and stimulating spiritually to do on Saturday nights. We began to go every Saturday night. Abdul Rashid would tell us wonderful things about Shaykh Nazim and he gave me a book entitled *Mercy Oceans* which I call "the green book" due to the color of its cover. Once I read *Mercy Oceans*, I was hooked. I wanted to be initiated then and there and I did so. Br. Abdul Haqq, the leader of the remembrance of God liturgy, initiated me. My sons and I have attended the gathering every Saturday if we are not traveling or ill.

As soon as I was financially able to do so, my sons and I traveled to London during Ramadan to actually meet Shaykh Nazim. We took their grandmother, sister Jamila, the mother of my ex-husband and a very dear friend. Both sister Jamila and I had been searching for spiritual development. It felt right to be a part of the Naqshbandi Sufi order; this was confirmed when we went to London. Both of us knew that was where we belonged. It is where we were meant to be. Both of us renewed our initiation personally with Shaykh Nazim and we were determined to do whatever we could to help the Naqshbandi Sufi order in Chicago grow.

I told my sons, however, as they were growing up that they could not assume Islam as a birth right and that I would not assume that they were in fact going to be Muslims merely because I raised them in Islam. I told them that it would be necessary for them to make that commitment on their own behalf if they wished to do so. I felt that age fifteen or sixteen was a good age to make a commitment of that magnitude. On that first trip to London, however, they were just thirteen yet they not only bore witness to the oneness of God and the messengership of Prophet Muhammad, peace and the blessings of God be upon him, but they were also initiated by Shaykh Nazim into the Naqshbandi Sufi order. I was astounded really. I had not expected that they would make that commitment at that early age but they elected to do so. As I was unmarried at the time, when I had an opportunity to speak with Shaykh Nazim, I explained to him that because I was unmarried, I wanted him to spiritually help me raise my sons. I basically gave my sons over to his care. I truly believe that being members of the Naqshbandi Sufi order is in large part what has kept my sons as interested as they are in being Muslim and evolving spiritually.

Sufism makes submitting to God's Will a living force for all of us. It is not just books and doctrine and rituals. It is a living force. It is something that we live day to day. We see things through the eyes of an ever changing, ever expanding consciousness. The Quran becomes alive for us. The Traditions become alive for us. These are concepts we can apply in our daily lives because we have a community of peers for support. We have the heartfelt understanding of what we are supposed to do, not supposed to do and why. We can be open, compassionate and loving to everyone regardless of sex, race, nationality, even religion. We can love everybody often in spite of themselves.

While we want everybody to revert to submission to God's Will and we encourage them to do so, we know too that there is no compulsion in religion. We are taught that the best way of attracting people is by example. If they see that we are peaceful, happy, loving and successful, they will want what we have. The only way they can get it is the way that we got it so they will come to the faith.

Basically I feel the bottom line is that God Almighty decreed that I should commit to inner change in no uncertain terms a very long time ago, and when I was ready God in His perfect knowledge brought me to the Naqshbandi order and that is where I have been ever since. God willing, that is where I will remain because it is Sufism that put Islam in my heart as well as my mind.

PART III
CONSCIOUSLY RETURNING TO GOD

Chapter 3: Turning Away From Anything Other Than God

Avoiding Vices
The Harms of Hypocrisy

Once we accept the belief that God is one, we are no longer considered by Sufis to be a disbeliever in God or a polytheist who worships more gods than there are, as it were. That is, by accepting the existence of God, we become believers. By accepting God's oneness, we become monotheists rather than polytheists. We first manifest this at the external level.

The internal level, the inner struggle with the self, comes next, and it is a war that continues throughout our lifetime. The battle is a long one because of the persistence of the ego or nurtured self. Our ego is considered to be a satanic force within because it is our ego which veils us from God. The ego develops through the socialization as something that separates us or veils us from God. The ego offers great resistance to turning away from anything other than God. The resistance, in effect, prevents us from becoming balanced, centered.

One of the greatest barriers that we have to turn

away from in order to return to our original natural balanced state is the temptation towards hypocrisy—saying with one's tongue that which one does not believe with one's heart.

Shah Waliullah describes three types of hypocrites, people who may or may not be aware of this moral imbalance within. It is his view, in particular, and the view of Sufism, in general, that the way to defeat the ego's resistance to real change is through following the Law. While following the Law may itself be an act of hypocrisy in that we pretend to be 'religious', it also provides a framework for both outward and inward change for those whose hearts are pure.

If a person is dominated by her own evil and harmful actions, she is a scoundrel but if her evil and corrupt characteristics become even stronger, then such a person is called a hypocrite since her actions are never free from hypocrisy....[22]

He refers to a Tradition in which the Prophet defined hypocrisy:

The Prophet has clearly indicated the characteristics of hypocrites. For example, he has said, 'That person in whom these three things are found is a pure hypocrite: first, when she makes a promise, she does not fulfill it. Second, when she disputes with someone, she becomes abusive. Third, when something is entrusted to her, she betrays the trust.'[23]

According to this definition of the Prophet, all seven women profiled here, who, after accepting submission to God's Will committed themselves to inner change, have made a promise to themselves and to their Creator, a promise to submit to God's Will. In their own words, they are keeping that promise in spite of external opposition.

Following the virtues they manifest, they would clearly not become abusive if someone were to dispute with them—although we have no textual evidence of this. Finally, they accepted commitment to inner change through the allegiance they gave to a living shaykh. They have not betrayed that trust. They accepted the trust and began working on themselves. They purified themselves instead of either allowing their egos to resist change or continuing to "shop around" to see what else is out there. This commitment on their part to both submission to God's Will and the esoteric dimension of commitment to inner change have allowed them to escape the chains of hypocrisy.

Shah Waliullah describes three types of hypocrites among who are those who claim to have submitted to God's Will but who go against their primordial nature of submission and who pretend to submit to God's Will but whose hearts are sealed.

Avoiding Imbalance

Lust Strong, Anger and Reason Weak

First, there is the type of person who is ruled by her physical energy and carnal self. Both her heart and her reason are subservient to these. By nature such a person goes wherever she likes without the permission of the Law or reason. She does whatever she wishes. She becomes involved in love affairs even though reason and the Law forbid it. If she is held up to shame by conventional standards, she pays this no heed and acts as if she is exempted from the Law and from popular retribution. She always produces some excuse for her behavior and uses this to drive out any thought of the Law, a vestige of which may lurk in the back of her mind. God describes such a hypocrite as deceitful in the Quran, *'They try to deceive God, but He deceives them'* (4:142). Elsewhere there is reference to their *'twisted breasts,'* (11:5). By breast is meant the knowledge of the breast and the twisting of it means that the hypocrite covers the thought of truth with the thought of untruth and thereby twists her knowledge into ignorance.

Sometimes this type of hypocrite sinks even lower than this and does not take the slightest note of the Law, being entirely satisfied with her unspoken justifications—although at times conflict and contradiction may flare up in her breast. Or, worse, she may hold firmly to her sense of license and become totally indifferent to the prohibition of the Law. Occasionally she may sink to the lowest level of all and actually begin to take pride in her sin and try to demonstrate its beauty. In this instance, as God has said, *'Their sin has encompassed them. They are the companions of the fire and will remain there forever'* (2:81).

A person of this type plunges herself into such indulgences as gluttony, alcohol, consumption and gambling. She enjoys ease and fine living. She forever craves the meaningless luxuries promoted by her [consumer] society. The very thought of acquiring showy [status-enhancing] possessions gives her pleasure. Her heart takes delight in seeking them. Even her reason is likewise engaged [compulsively] in striving for them. She is angry with those who criticize such activities and takes as her friend whoever approves of her pursuits. She shows aversion towards everything which tends to keep her away from her pleasures. Yet, where friendship is concerned, she spends her wealth lavishly and gives freely of herself to help any friend in need. Conversely, if she has occasion to show hatred, she thinks nothing of abusing, striking or even killing the offending person. She may keep a grudge concealed for a long time but in the end it will come into the open. Her intellect uses every possible device to conjure up this image of pleasure and to think up stratagems to obtain it. It removes any obstacles from her path and grants her freedom to do anything she might consider herself unable to do.

ANGER RULES, LUST AND REASON GIVE SUPPORT

The second type of hypocrite is one whose heart energies are excessive with the result that natural lust and reason are neglected. Such a person is constantly engaged in gaining dominance over her fellows and revenging herself on those who put up any resistance. She can conceal a grudge for a long time and is continuously thinking of killing, striking, overthrowing or humiliating her adversaries. She accepts those who defer to her and seeks to overthrow anyone who happens to be her equal. The slightest word is enough to make her lose her temper and declare that she is not the sort of person who can accept any dishonor or threat—[an attempt to maintain her "image', both in her own mind and in that of others]. In this respect her natural lust obeys her heart and reason assists her. She is prepared to tolerate any hardship if she can thereby give practical expression to her anger. With the greatest ease she devises plans to show her rancor and revenge.

Sometimes, on the other hand, she may be seized with such a degree of friendship for people or attachment to a custom that she strives valiantly on their behalf without considering the prohibitions of Law and reason. It is an essential feature of her conduct that she tries to remain loyal to her friends. It is an inherent part of her constitution to abide by her own customs. She is not one of those creatures who can change friends and customs from one moment to the next. In the opinion of the uninformed, such people with a marked aggressive drive, are truly strong and superior to those who are driven by feelings of natural lust.[24]

ABILITY TO REASON TOO STRONG OR TOO WEAK

The third type of hypocrite is one whose reason is confused. Or perhaps her reason may be sound, but she has nonetheless fallen into some sort of error—such as believing that God has a body or ascribing human attributes to God or believing that God does not have any attributes, etc. Or she may entertain doubts concerning the Koran or the Prophet or the future life, without ever having gone so far as to be declared an apostate.

Alternatively, the situation may be that her intelligence has been overrun by dark oppressive thoughts so that she is no longer convinced about anything and is thus unable to bring her intentions to any sort of conclusion. Or it may be that she has gone too deeply into poetry or mathematics and thus failed to give sufficiently deep thought to the Law.[25]

Thus there are basically three types of hypocrites but owing to the fact that the three types may be mixed together in varying combinations depending on the context and activity in question, there are ultimately innumerable types. The remedy established by the Lawgiver for these various types of hypocrite is that they should live in such a way that their reason should control their natural anger located in the heart and the heart should control their natural lust located in the liver or gut. Each of these controls is maintained by appropriate actions.[26]

DISCIPLINING THE ANIMAL ENERGIES WITHIN

Being careful to avoid the pitfall of hypocrisy, the seeker works on turning away from the animal energies of lust (at other levels referred to as attraction to pleasure, concupiscence or preserving the species) and anger (at other levels referred to as avoidance of harm, irascible or preserving the individual).

The purpose of self-purification is to decrease the effects of the animal energies. Controlling the animal energies within means eliminating the negative traits or vices built up through the nurturing process.

The negative traits arise because of an excess or deficiency in the naturally pure state. There are three natural functions: attraction to pleasure, avoidance of harm and reason. An excess of attraction to pleasure leads to certain negative traits in terms of quantity just as does a deficiency in it. The same is true of avoidance of harm and reason.

Quantitative Imbalance
Signs of Too Much Too Much Lust

When our natural lust or species-preserving function is too strong, we become greedy, covetous and extravagant. We accept debased aspirations and hopes. We develop gluttony and hoard what we have. We may become impudent and licentious as we develop loss of self-respect. Love of the world, wealth and riches leads to inappropriate lusting for more. We become overbearing and prodigal, self-indulgent and shameless. As status seekers, we are wasteful spendthrifts who squander our blessings and end only by increasing our endless emptiness.

Signs of Too Little Lust

Signs of a deficiency in our natural lust are apathy in regard to food, sex and work. We begrudge others whatever they have and yet are complacent about what we lack. We fall into despair, impassively indifferent to what is going on around us. We lack zest, becoming miserly and obstinate as we retreat from life. We exercise neurotic self-restraint, are lazy, unemotional and unsociable.

Signs of Too Much Anger

If we have an excess of the natural faculty of anger necessary to preserve the species, we develop recklessness and violent behavior. Our inappropriate anger results in quarrelsomeness and we become argumentative. Arrogant and conceited, we develop enmity towards others. We become fanatic in our views, hard-hearted, harsh and hasty. Hostile towards others, we are ill-tempered, impatient and irritable. We use foul language. Inflated with pride, we become selfish and vengeful, treacherous troublemakers who are jealous, vain and judgmental.

SIGNS OF TOO LITTLE ANGER

On the other hand, when our natural ability to avoid harm is too weak, we lack the necessary strength we need to preserve our individuality. We become bashful and unassertive, cowardly and lacking in a sense of dignity. Fainthearted, we accept our own humiliation and that of our family. We may have an inferiority complex which causes us to be self-deprecating and lacking in self-confidence. Lacking self-esteem, we become spiritless and timid.

SIGNS OF TOO MUCH REASON

If our natural reasoning abilities become too strong, we become crafty and cunning, sly and wily, deceitful, dry and full of doubts. We are contemptuous of the opinion of other people and use excessive argument to make a point. We make false promises indicating our state of hypocrisy. We lie and slander. We are malicious and intellectually ostentatious, overconscious of self, showing off to others and too detached from the immediacy of life.

SIGNS OF TOO LITTLE REASON

When our natural reasoning abilities are deficient, we show signs of mistrust, polytheism and ignorance. We are prejudiced and easily influenced by satanic temptations. We are unable to discriminate.

QUALITATIVE IMBALANCE
SIGNS OF DEPRAVITY OF LUST, ANGER OR REASON

Too much or too little lust, anger or reason result in an excess or deficiency in terms of quantity. There are yet three other negative states (one for each of the three functions) which result from a total depravity within the conditioned or nurtured state. This is a qualitative lack within the nurtured state.

A depravity, not just a deficiency, in our ability to

preserve the species, manifests itself in the negative traits of envy, backbiting, excessive grief and a sense of purposelessness.

Depravity in the function of neurotic self-preservation or avoidance of harm manifests itself as fear of anything other than God, delight in the misfortunes of others and tolerating injustice.

When it comes to our natural ability to reason, it, too, may be in a state of depravity resulting in atheism, disbelief, and/or fatalism. It is a state in which the defense mechanisms which serve the animal energies thrive. Such mechanisms include: projection, denial, introjection, regression, acting out, repression, rationalization, displacement, intellectualization, reaction formation and isolation.

According to Shah Waliullah, our guide throughout this study, either animal energies prevail or they are somewhat subdued by angelic energies. The third possibility he refers to—the angelic energies succeed in controlling the animal energies—will be taken up in the next chapter.

In amplification of this we can say that when the angelic energy is in conflict with the animal energy, the outcome is bound to be one of three situations:

Either the animal energy will prevail and the angelic energy will be subdued to such an extent as not to be in evidence at all—except on certain occasions and even then it will be far from pleased with its own particular attributes....

Alternatively the angelic energy may have the animal energy firmly by the neck, but the latter still has its hands and feet free to continue the struggle. As long as the angelic energy does not slacken its grip and withdraw from the fight, such a person is called a companion of the right hand side.

There are two possible explanations for the persistence of excessive or deficient attraction to pleasure for this world in this situation: on the one hand, either the excess or deficiency of the energy of avoidance of harm or reason may be inherently too little or too much causing it to be weak. Such a person may perform many good actions, but the desired benefit of such actions cannot be realized. On the other hand, these energies may have been created in a sound condition within her and yet she has failed to perform many good actions, having become dominated by her concern for her daily bread.[27]

This process of controlling the negative effects of too much, too little or depravity in the nurtured state, according to Shah Waliullah in his *Altaf al-Quds*, has a remedy. In his words,

"The remedy (to release the self from the animal energies) is called the Law..."[28]

The final purpose of this remedy

....is to achieve deliverance from the wrongs done among the people of this world, from the punishment of the grave and the Day of Judgment... [because] the Prophet said that people should avoid wrongdoing and act in such a way as to escape the punishment of the grave and Judgment Day. Whoever thinks otherwise has not understood the Prophet's aims, strategies, commands and prohibitions...[29]

He further adds to this point by referring to the famous Tradition of the Prophet that everyone is born in submission to God's Will, but that the nurturing environment changes this.

Essentially the Law is in accord with a balanced natural disposition. This point is made clear in the Tradition in which the Prophet says, 'There is no one who is not born according to nature. It is one's parents who make of one a Jew, a Christian or a Zoroastrian. The young of animals are not born with slit ears or noses'.[30]

This is the remedy sought by all seven Sufi women profiled here.

SUFI WOMEN

HODA

For seventeen years Shaykh Nazim both directly and through his representative in North America, Shaykh Hisham Kabbani, has provided an inspired understanding of the Quran and the *Sunnah* (sayings and deeds of Prophet Muhammad) as well as an example of surrender so complete that the scrupulous observance of the Divine Law has become for him spontaneous, effortless, fresh and utterly natural. His attunement to God's Will and His progressively unfolding design are so perfect that, although outwardly still possessing a highly adaptive personality, inwardly he has become an unbounded area of service, a path everyone can walk on, a mercy ocean. To me the experience of being a Sufi woman is inextricably bound to his example.

LATIFA

Part of the way that women are viewed in Islam, part of the misconception, stems from a misreading of the Divine Law by either those who have submitted to God's Will or those who have not. If they were to study the life of the Prophet, peace be upon him, they would never behave that way.... If they used the example of the Prophet, there would not be this misconception.

ALIYA

The Naqshbandi disciples here in North America are leaving everything for Islam. This is very true. When we accept Islam so often our parents and our family, even husbands and wives, our relationships are often torn apart by accepting Islam.

KHADIJA

When you submit to the guidance of a shaykh, a true shaykh with divine connections, one who follows the Divine

Law, your life begins to change.

RASHEEDAH

My husband, Dawud, stressed common sense submission to the Will of God. He stressed the spirit of the Law and understanding of the spirit of the Law so that one can better understand the letter of the Law. This has always been my philosophy of life. If a thing does not make sense to me, it is pretty difficult for me to adhere to it. If I don't understand why and how it fits into the overall scheme of things, it is real difficult for me to relate to it.

BAGHA

At the age of twenty I came to know that most of the time our desire for physical pleasure is stronger than the pleasure itself. By calming our mind and transmuting mundane pleasures into more refined ones, they become more pleasant, purer with little waste or pollution.

HAJJA NAZIHE

I missed my father a great deal because he was always traveling for the sake of Islam and Sufism. My mother never complained. Sometimes my mother was pregnant and would give birth to my brother or sister and my father would return three or four months after the child was born. My mother never complained because she knew that her husband was helping to propagate submission to God's Will. My mother was like both father and mother because she raised us alone when my father traveled. She raised us according to Divine Law.

The first time I came to America I was unhappy. I felt that I had been living in a paradise. I did not find that here. I had been living and moving between the mosque and the Sufi center. I did not find this. The sound of the call to prescribed prayer in the minaret near our home, the recitation of blessings on the Prophet, invocation of God's Names here and there, recitation of celebration of the birthday of the Prophet, like they do in Lebanon at evening time. This is why I regretted coming here the first couple of years. Bearing it patiently, I began to meet more Muslim women to whom I could relate. This opened a new life for me. They have made me feel just like I felt in Lebanon.

Thus we see that all seven Sufi women have sought out what Shah Waliullah calls the remedy—the Law. While Hajja Nazihe and Bagha were raised with it, the other five voluntarily accepted it because the models they follow accept it. They are intuitively aware of the fact that there are angelic energies available through this remedy as opposed to the support for animal energies offered by the material, phenomenal world.

HOLDING ANIMAL ENERGIES IN CHECK

From the words of the women interviewed, we see they have moved away from the negative influence of vices towards the positive virtues by subduing and disciplining their egos.

While Khadija used to catch herself backbiting, she no longer does so. Hoda may say she is a liar but she is referring to lying to herself in order to force herself to change, to become that which she really wishes to be. Latifa speaks of her doubts in her faith while Bagha speaks of her confusion. Both sensed certainty when they choose commitment to inner change.

None of them refers to a love of wealth and riches as a goal in her life. None craves the expensive consumer items taunted as necessities by the mass media. If wealth is there, fine, but it is not something they eagerly seek.

Rather, what they seek is inner peace. Five came from a religious background—we do not learn about Khadija and Hoda's early childhood. Rasheedah clearly grew up in an environment which stressed the importance of reason. Six of them speak of their persistence, their searching and their questioning. Throughout this search they remained responsible single parents always concerned for significant others. As Hajja Nazihe grew up in an intellectual environment where commitment to inner change was continuously discussed and had role models who had subdued their own egos, she is able to remain closer to the pure state in which we are all born. The other sisters had to go through strenuous endeavor and struggle to tap into at least some of the same angelic energies.

Chapter 4: Turning Towards the One God

Attracting Virtues

When we are balanced, when our psychic constituents are harmoniously integrated, we manifest the angelic energies of the virtues. While there are hundreds of virtues, traditional psychology has organized them under four classical headings of temperance, courage, wisdom and justice.

While temperance is the balancing of attraction to pleasure (concupiscence), courage is the balancing of avoiding pain (irascible) and reason is the balancing of preserving the eternal possibility of self. If balance has in fact been attained, proof of balance is the appearance of the fourth classical virtue, justice. The appearance of the proof of justice, however, is only visible to others outside ourselves. The angelic energies arise out of our counseling ourselves to virtues as pleasures and preventing vices from developing.

Shah Waliullah speaks of the virtues of temperance, courage and wisdom (when held in balance) as culminating in justice, attained through that self-purification which begins with following the Law.

The strategy of the Law with regard to the foregoing is developed in two direction. The first involves effecting a reformation through good deeds, the abandonment of the major sins, and the establishment of the marks of true religion. For these three things, observances and limits are laid down. All followers of the Law are required to abide by them. This is the outward form of the Law and is called submission to God's Will.

The second direction consists in the purification of the various selves through the reality of the four virtues, passing from these forms of goodness to the splendors which they contain and progressing from the mere outward abstention from sin to a repudiation of its very essence. This is the inward form of the Law and it is called [commitment to change].[31]

Traditional psychology classifies virtues as the active three types of temperance, courage and wisdom as well as the potential virtue of justice—potential because it only appears when the other three are present. The virtues included in this triad come from God's Most Beautiful Names which are traditionally 99 in number. The names of temperance are those Qualities revealed to creation. The names of courage are those Qualities revealed to humanity while the names of wisdom are those qualities revealed to Self. While God alone contains the infinite Names and Qualities in the Absolute sense, each one of us can only assume them as virtues in their relative or contingent sense, with the further condition that within us they can operate as virtues only when we are egoless, i.e. free of animal energies. If they are assumed in the satanic state of egocentricity or arrogance, they become vices rather than virtues, animal rather than angelic.

Shah Waliullah then describes the interaction of the four classical virtues:

God has drawn the human being's attention towards the cultivation of four cardinal virtues. If you think carefully, you will find that all kinds of goodness are merely an elaboration of these four virtues; conversely, all types of sin are merely an elaboration of their opposite characteristics. These four virtues are precisely the ones which all the prophets have exhorted the people to imbibe. There can be no question of any change or abrogation with regard to these virtues. If there is any difference in what the various Lawgivers say about them, this is only a matter of their outward form, not their real substance.

The first virtue is wisdom. Through this the human being is related to the angels. The second is courage by means of which the human being acquires an affinity with the exalted assembly. The third is liberality or temperance, generosity. By cultivating this quality, the human being wipes out the stains left by base human nature such as the actions of animality and lust still firmly rooted in his or her rational soul. The fourth virtue is justice. It is through justice that a person may be pleasing in the sight of the exalted assembly, may gain favor with it and receive its mercy and blessings.[32]

FROM LUST TO TEMPERANCE

Replacing vices obtained through the nurturing process, we cultivate the virtues of the Names revealed to creation, thereby moving towards the naturally pure state of each and every one of God's creatures whether seen—stars, planets, minerals, plants, and animals—or unseen—angels and good jinn. This we may do traditionally through the names, qualities or attributes as they appear in seven stages, the order of which may vary. Transforming natural lust into temperance is expressed as moving through the divine attributes (appearing in italics) in seven stages of resolve (submission), hope-fear, piety, moderation, tranquility, spiritual poverty, and self-restraint. The words in italics are the relative form of a divine attribute.

Resolve (submission): *Compelling* the natural energy of lust to listen to reason, strengthening the attraction to pleasure to turn consciously towards the threefold creative process of the *creator* within and give birth to the nature originated by God—creator of self *in perfect harmony*—*balanced*—*shaper of unique inward beauty*.

Hope-Fear: As *constrictor*, we limit fear to fearing God alone and as *expander*, we place our hope and trust in God alone. We *exalt* God and *abase* self, *honor* what God honors and *dishonor* what God dishonors.

Piety: We guard and *preserve* our appropriate desires by counseling ourself to balance, *appraising* our deeds in order to *resurrect* our nature originated by God.

Moderation: From the *beginning* of our commitment to inner changes, we seek to *restore* our spiritual heart, *give life* to it as we strive to *slay* our false self or ego.

Tranquility: Enhancing our *spiritual power*, we *promote* our spiritual heart and *postpone* our desires for pleasure.

Spiritual Poverty: We *govern* our attraction to pleasure through avoiding harm, letting our reason rule as *king, sovereign* over us. We treat ourselves in an *equitable* way, *gathering* our positive traits under the umbrella of spiritual poverty.

Self-Restraint: Enhancing self-restraint through control of our desires, we become *protectors* of our self from worldly harms and final *punishment*, recognizing what is *beneficial* so that when God *inherits* our remains, we return to God *right in guidance*.

From Anger to Courage

Disciplining the natural ability to preserve the individual (anger, avoidance of harm) we move through seven traditional stages although, again, the order may vary. The seven stags are compassion, moral reasonableness, thankfulness, vigilance, trust and repentance.

Compassion: Natural anger is modified through developing *compassion* and *mercy* towards others, acting as *believers* in and *guardians* of the nature originated by God. Along with compassion and mercy comes *forgiveness* of self and others. The sign of God's forgiveness of us in the view of traditional psychology is when we no longer do what we had asked to be forgiven for.

Moral Reasonableness: Establishing moral reasonableness comes from recognizing God as the *bestower* and *provider*, praying for God to *open* our hearts to the greatness bestowed upon us, showing *forbearance* when things do not work out the way we want them to. Armed with forbearance and the willingness to *conceal the faults of others,* we realize that there is a bigger picture, a greater universal design we may not understand.

Thankfulness: Natural anger is n*ourished* and moved towards the development of courage through *thankfulness* to our maintainer who maintains us even before we ask. We reckon our blessings and give to others of our time and effort.

Vigilance: Being *vigilant* we become aware of the fact that God sees us even if we do not see God. As *devotees, loving* our Creator, we *bear witness* to the creation.

Trustee, Friend: Accepting the *trust* of God's creation of nature, we become its *friend* and protector.

Repentance: As *repenters* and *pardoners* of our mistakes we maintain the balance by acting with a *vengeance* to control inappropriate anger.

Patience: This teaches us *patience* as we become *clement* towards ourselves, *enrich* our lives by developing our full potential under the direction of an inner and/or outer *guide*.

FROM REASON TO WISDOM

Strengthening natural reason also occurs through seven stages: aspiration, self-examination and consciousness, truthfulness, contentment, unity/constancy, sincerity and remembrance.

Aspiration: Aspiring to balance we become *sovereigns* of the animal energies within. A sense of *sacred* self develops which moves towards *flawlessness*, each individual being *incomparable* in some sense to the next. Having controlled our anger by letting go of false *pride*, we *subdue* our anger, listening to the angelic energies speaking to us through our reasoning abilities.

Self-Examination, Consciousness: We continuously self-examine: Is there more I need to *know*? Am I *hearing* what others are saying to me? Am I *seeing* myself as others see me? When do I need to *arbitrate* between my animal energies in order to control my compulsions? Am I being fair and *just* to myself? Are there *subtle* imbalances of which I am not *aware*?

Truthfulness: Am I able to rise above the material, phenomenal, relative world and come in touch with the *magnificent* aspects of self given to me by God? Have I been fair to God's *greatness* and *majesty*, the *vastness* and *generosity* of God's creation, the underlying *wisdom* in it and the *glory* of *Truth*?

Concealment: Reason becomes content when it is *strong* and *firm*. It is then able to *praise* others, *living* independently as if *self-existing* while knowing all along that every thing is dependent upon Other and becoming *resourceful* while assuming the *noble* character traits.

Unity/Constancy: Once we recognize the *Unique One* Who alone is *Eternal* then we are *enabled* to fulfill our destiny as true servants of God.

Sincerity: Then we can say in all sincerity that God is the *First*, the *Last*, the *Manifest* and the *Hidden*.

Remembrance: It is then that we remember God as the *Exalted*, the *Source of All Goodness*, the *Lord of Majesty and Generosity*, the only one who is truly *Rich*, the *Light* of the heavens and the earth, the *Originator* of all creation and the only one who is *Everlasting*.

Each of the seven women exhibited the positive

traits of temperance, courage and wisdom resulting in a sense of fairness or justice in both a qualitative and quantitative sense.

Hoda and Latifa, manifesting a strong cognitive function, move towards attaining the virtue of wisdom while Bagha, Aliya and Khadija move towards attaining courage as the strength of their strong behavioral function. Yet each has been able to balance their other two aspects of self through her strongest function. Hoda showed great courage by going to Damascus in 1978 by her self, and both she and Latifa had the courage to leave husbands who either did not practice Islam or whose Islamic practices were overgrown with cultural rather than religious accretions. Bagha showed courage by running a day care school in the midst of a war. Aliya and Khadija's courage to choose Islam resulted in Aliya's daughter accepting Islam and in Khadija's mother's conversion. Rasheedah mentions that from an early age she loved long dresses and scarves showing her development of temperance. All three were also single parents, as were Hoda and Latifa. They continued to search, as did Hoda, Bagha and Latifa, for a guide showing the signs of the presence of wisdom. All six manifest temperance as well through their desire to serve others, their sense of generosity, their roles as teachers and volunteers in Islamic schools.

The attainment of balancing these positive traits in the Islamic perspective needs to be confirmed and validated by another, showing how here society is prior to the individual. When allowed to speak about how becoming a Sufi woman has changed their lives, if at all, all seven spoke more about other people than themselves. Bagha spoke about her experiences with Sufi shaykhs. Hoda spoke about Shaykh Nazim and her children. Latifa spoke about Hajja Nazihe. Aliya spoke about Nigerian and Cypriate friends, about Shaykh Nazim, about Shaykh Hisham and his family as well as her own daughter. Khadija spoke about another Sufi woman who became a role model for her, about Shaykh Hisham and his family and about her mother. Hajja Nazihe spoke about her father, mother, husband and children.

They are, then, able to put things in their rightful place by situating themselves in relation to others and by emphasizing the importance of others as contributors to their own growth, rather than taking credit themselves for their positive traits. Hoda was very hard on herself in an attempt to be what Latifa spoke about—self-effacing. Latifa was able to move out of two unsupportive marital situations as was Aliya and Khadija. Latifa and Aliya felt an honest relationship was more important as a model for their children than staying and being abused. They also spoke about the ego being tested and the importance of self-effacement as well.

While Hajja Nazihe manifests having attained a level of balance by experiencing grief over the death of her adopted grandfather, Grandshaykh Abdullah ad-Daghestani, and by the joy and happiness of serving others, she is confirmed by another as being balanced in wisdom, temperance and courage, and as attaining the virtue of justice or fairness. This latter virtue is seen as "putting everything in its rightful place," through continuous centering.

SUFI WOMEN

HODA

To me being a Sufi woman means using my special God-given sensitivities to do God's will as expressed in the rich and multifaceted Islamic tradition. This means following shaykhs Nazim and Hisham in both their inspired understanding and their immense scholarly knowledge of the Quran. It also means failing a lot. It means a glimpse of how heedless, stale and uncharitable my actions often are. It means facing the fact that on a deep level, I am a liar. But it also means the hope that the false face, the negatively conditioned face that I identify as myself will finally wear away and basic sincerity will step through and blossom and replace the old rattling shell of hypocrisy. It means hope that some day, by God's grace, real life will quicken in me, real religion, real love, real goodness. Until then there is patience and practice, and the sheer paradoxical beauty of even a mediocre life. Until then there is listening to the hidden wordless song of the heart slowly transforming itself into a diamond, a diamond shining in the black, glittering abyss of the Absolute. And like the song says particularly for Sufi women, diamonds are a girl's best friend.

LATIFA

Last year Shaykh Hisham asked me (an academic) to work with his wife. I had a momentary pang of, 'But I won't get to hear him speak,' not realizing how much I was going to learn from her. In addition to the wonderful lessons I learned from her, one of the biggest lessons was that when he finishes being the shaykh in front of his disciples, when he finishes his shaykhly duties outside the house, he comes in the house and picks up a knife or spoon and continues to work beside her until her job is finished. Then the two of them sit down together and have a cup of coffee. It is this misinterpretation by people that is responsible for the misinterpretation of the role of women.

ALIYA

I realized that the great inheritors of the Prophet, these great saints are bringing submission to the Will of God even though I am not at a level where I can understand a lot of it. They are bringing enough to my heart and to people like me to want to be around the shaykhs. Even though we may not be disciples, we are brothers and sisters of the Sufi path. People who love the shaykh, who love submission to God's Will, who want to be around the shaykh, were so happy to understand that God's religion is not dead. It is alive and it is carried in the whole experience of submission to God's Will to people in their life. I was able to be around it and to see it, to feel it and to taste it, to experience this submission.

Our shaykhs tell us that Sufism is a taste, it is an experience and that's it. It makes the heart alive again. This is a new birth, a new initiation, a new level of submission even for those who have been practicing the Divine Law. They tell us if one follows the Divine Law, eventually that person will be lead to the Path or Sufism. The ethics of submission, the excellent practice of it, praise belongs to God, I'm telling you that with my humble understanding of religion, I do not consider myself to be anything special even in the little practice that I was able to grasp. I just feel so blessed to even be considered to be one who would be around those who are trying to learn this other level of submission to God's Will, the development of good character, the purity, the excellent practice, the good performance of submission.

We are learning from our shaykhs that submission to God's Will has various levels. After one bears witness to the oneness of God and the messengership of Muhammad, peace and the mercy of God be upon him, and begins to practice the five daily prescribed prayers, begins to understand the basic principles of the belief, then there is another level that one can be introduced to through the power of good teachers, through the power of seeing, and this is what we are experiencing in the Naqshbandi Order through our great line of saints, of grandshaykhs in the order all the way back to Abu Bakr as-Siddiq. It is very difficult to describe the experience because you understand how blessed you are to be considered for such initiation and such teachings and such instructions, to be worthy to get this instruction.

KHADIJA

I think shaykh is showing us that this is how the world should be. There is a microcosm of people: French, Indo-Pakistani, all these wonderful myriad of types, all living together, cooking together, working together and getting along. I feel that shaykh is monitoring this and that we are playing house with the world. This is how it is supposed to be.

Rasheedah

As Sufism stresses putting our egos in submission rather than being their slaves, often times I think that while we may be behaving or thinking in ways that are less than truly representative of submission to God's Will, we are, at least, aware of that fact. I think Sufism makes us all more aware of the tricks that our egos play on us. There are times, I am sure, at least for me and probably for everyone else, when we know our ego is in control. We just cannot or will not stop it, but at least we are increasingly aware of this. I look at other people. I watch their interactions with one another individually and collectively. I see these egos running rampant, butting heads like two rams. It saddens me that they do not understand that it is their egos, in fact, which are being so confrontational, arrogant and ignorant. It is the promptings of their egos and not their essential nature to behave in that way. Because they do not realize it, they do not take steps to alter it and it goes on and on.

Bagha

Later when I noticed Shaykh Hisham's intellectual, social, communal creative and persevering hard work, I found out that his being on earth is a great blessing for humanity, especially considering the scale and extent of his difficult job. There is no question for me that shaykh's extraordinary ability to undertake huge tasks comes from the Divine Source. Shaykh Hisham's external simplicity and accessibility are as natural as his deep access to inner wisdom. Courage and kindness and patience decorate him all the time. I need to add this here, that Hajja Nazihe's heart's purity is so present that words are too limited to describe her message. She is an able heart-healer through the remembrance of God.

Hajja Nazihe

My love for Grandshaykh Abd Allah al-Daghestani was so great because I was raised by him in the company of many intellectual people. I was so sad when Grandshaykh died. It was as if I had lost both my parents at the same time. My love was so great for him because he raised me. I felt the loss for many years. It was like a paradise being with him because Grandshaykh's home and my father's house was never empty of people. I met many people. Many times Grandshaykh gave me water to drink and it tasted sweeter than honey. I had never tasted such water. Dried bread in his house was better than all the food elsewhere. That experience is only tasted when you live it and see how sweet it is to live with saints. Everything was tasty to me. My mother is a wonderful example. She cooks for 100-200 people every day. She never changes the way of cooking. There is a kind of spirituality that is mixed with the food and the love and happiness because [as she cooks] she praises the Prophet or recites invocations like 'praise be to God,' or 'God is Greater'. Or she may be reciting the Quran as she cooks. This is how I have been raised. Not shouting, 'Give me the knife, the fork, the spoon, etc.' My mother always has ablution when she cooks and she is in a state in the remembrance of God.

THE APPEARANCE OF THE ANGELIC ENERGIES (JUSTICE)

Shah Waliullah has already described animal energies, as those energies that need to be controlled by a balanced sense of reason. Now he describes the angelic energies which through self-purification come to replace the negative animal energies.

[Another] situation is found when the angelic energy finally achieves victory and holds the excess or deficiency of attraction to pleasure in close captivity, shattering its base desires and keeping it permanently starved. Such a person is called 'foremost of those who are near to God'. In the case of this latter individual, two things are essential. First, her avoidance of harm and reason functions must have been created in a sound condition. Second, her reasoning must have been purified by the true articles of faith and must have managed to seize and subjugate the resolve of the heart (positive state). This power of resolve [stemming from the natural state of avoidance of harm] is then able to control lust. In this way the individual becomes entirely worthy of nearness to God.[33]

These sisters willingly adopted the remedy thereby becoming either those who follow the middle course or those who are foremost in good deeds based on the Quranic verse, *'Then We have given the Book for inheritance to such of our servants as we have chosen but there are among them some who wrong their own souls, some who follow a middle course, and some who are, by God's leave, foremost in good deeds. That is the highest grace'* (35:32).

Shah Waliullah says in regard to this verse,

Once the Law has prepared the people to adopt this strategy and has brought them to the point, willingly or otherwise, of putting it into practice, individuals differ widely in the extent to which they have accepted it because of their different dispositions and vocations. They thus inevitably fall into one of three categories-a point to which the Quran alludes.

What is required is that the human beings should adorn themselves with the angelic properties so that the angelic faculties may become stronger and so that the animal faculties may be trained in their ways and take on the coloring of the angelic faculties. However, this should not take place in such a way that the animal faculties become divested of their own nature, qualities and taste or that their reality is turned upside down.[34]

It is also clear that it is not a question of her innate nature for Shah Waliullah says,

Through hard exercise the nature of the self can be changed and it can be extricated from its own inherent constitution.[35]

He gives us the reason by saying, "Sufis have been given a balancing factor."[36] Hajja Nazihe, the one sister who grew up in a traditional Sufi nurturing system in which the egoless state of balance is constantly stressed and in which reason rules over innate lust and anger, arrived at balance at an age when the other Sufi women interviewed were still struggling to find balance.

While each of the seven Sufi women either saw or heard the angelic forces in others around them, one of the seven, Hajja Nazihe, was confirmed by another Sufi woman as actually manifesting angelic energy. Hoda was able to see the angelic energy as defined by Shah Waliullah, operative in Shaykh Nazim while Khadija saw it in a Sufi woman. Aliya heard the angels in the walls of the Sufi center in London, while Rasheedah heard them in the associations. Bagha had what might be described as an angelic experience and Hajja Nazihe, who is confirmed by Latifa as manifesting angelic energy herself, heard her father talking to the angels. This is how they describe it.

SUFI WOMEN

HODA

I knew Shaykh Muhammad Nazim was a real fountain for the thirsty, a fountain of truth, a fountain of clear, cool flame, a spring of silence. My life was changed by that simple, basic encounter with fundamental generosity. Through seventeen years of ups and downs, ins and outs, heres and theres, the only remotely comparable experience were the faces of my two children immediately after birth and the brilliance of a star strewn sky. For me Shaykh Nazim is a guidepost, a light house, a kind of living niche directing one to the Kabah, pointing the way from the sound and fury of egoic existence towards endless clarity, towards that which has no opposite, towards the absolutely Near, towards the God from whom we came and to whom, God willing, we will ultimately return.

Moreover, the shaykh, empty of ego, acts as a mirror who

simultaneously reflects and establishes my true self, my higher consciousness, the essential image of God lying within like forgotten treasure. For me the Sufism of my teacher makes submission to God's Will a contemporary reality by reactualizing such seminal events as the oath of allegiance given to the Prophet, peace be upon him, by his closest companions who thereby received deeper insights into Quranic truths.

Also in prayer and meditation the Sufi aspirant attempts to reinact the Prophet's spiritual ascent through a hierarchy of multiple meanings in his Night Journey. By the skillful use of such initiatory practices, the life and work of the Prophet ceases to be only a museum piece, a pious artifact, a dry well and becomes a living channel of holy understanding here and now, an endlessly refreshing encounter, a renewable resource, a most precious example of the world-sustaining balance between the inner and the outer dimensions, between detachment and compassion. Thus as a Sufi shaykh and his followers abandon themselves to the love of the Prophet they come to embody together the lock/key complementarity of the Law and the Love.

LATIFA

If you want to see self-effacement and tamed ego then you only have to look at Shaykh's wife. Most people do not even realize that she is there. She is easily half his strength. She is our example as women. She does this all day quietly and incredibly well. She is clearly supported by the highest power. She does this with graciousness and takes care of us and is constantly expressing humility. Her gentle teaching—the other day she was teaching me how to make seclusion soup.

Shaykh has taken an academic (me) and stuck her in the kitchen for the summer. It seems to be a brilliant move for now I'm learning the gentle lessons of Hajja Nazihe. She was teaching me how to make seclusion soup which was going to feed a large number of people with wholesome rice, lentils and onions. She not only taught me how to make the soup, which was to fulfill the people's need for sustenance in order to work and to pray, but she was also teaching me how this soup has been used traditionally in our Sufi order as the soup of choice for the shaykh and his disciples when they were in seclusion. She told me that her father (Shaykh Nazim) would have this soup once in every twenty-four hour period while he was in seclusion with perhaps a piece of bread. She went on from that story to tell of other stories of seclusions of other shaykhs and their significance. So I was given this wonderful, intimate teaching session that the men will never have.

Hajja Nazihe is constantly giving. Her house is never empty. She never has a quiet time. It would appear no time, almost no time alone or with family. Shaykh Hisham has told me that there are many women shaykhs in this order. Clearly his wife is a hidden treasure. She does not announce herself. There is no presentation of shaykh and shaykha but she is definitely a spiritual leader in her own right and as a Sufi woman, as a Muslim woman, I take my cue from her, I learn from her and she is an endless wealth.

Aliya

When we would rise in the morning for the morning pre-dawn breakfast [and the beginning of the fast] I could hear all kinds of sounds of invocation of God's Names coming from the walls. When we would start the morning Naqshbandi devotions, beautiful devotions involving the recitation of the prayer along with the recitation of the Quran, and the remembrance of God service, the special prayer and supplication that just goes on was reverberating throughout the entire mosque. Early morning we would stay in dawn prescribed prayer and then the early morning would come slowly, slowly, slowly. We would begin in darkness and end with just a little of the morning light.

Khadija

I noticed this beautiful mesa with this blue sky, cactus and this woman walking in her peasant garb and scarf tied under her chin. She had this beautiful radiant smile on her face. She waved at us with her prayer beads in her hand. I said to myself, 'Whatever that sister has, I want.' She just looked so peaceful—in the earth but not of the earth. I felt that I needed to find out what her secret was.

RASHEEDAH

The Naqshbandi Sufi order has undergone a number of transitions and changes. All of us have observed them in ourselves and in our brothers and sisters—astounding degrees of spiritual development. I am amazed at times at what Sufism has done not only in terms of our collective and individual spiritual development, but as regards the different types of people that have been reached; the different types of people whose hearts have been touched. One feels the true spirit of Islam exemplified as a result of meeting members of the order, people from all walks of life, very wealthy people, very poor people, people of African descent, people of European descent, people of Asian descent forming one Community based upon love and respect—knowledge and wisdom.

BAGHA

Ramadan of 1980 split my life into two distinct episodes. I like to call it *"waqhia"* which means the great event or the Day of Judgment.

It was evening on one of the last days of the month of prescribed fast. I was reading the Quran in my room just before breaking the fast. Suddenly I found myself on the ceiling of my day care's office. I saw my physical being sitting on the chair behind the desk. Immediately I knew that it was the time for farewell. I had to detach myself from everyone and everything. The urge to leave was super powerful. The last and hardest thing was to forget about my daughter. I was confused about how to leave her behind, but the pull was stronger than any wish. All the efforts to detach myself, all anxieties, all apologies took only three short seconds. From the top of my office I started my unusual trip. I had become light-like vapor, extremely energetic, conscious and free. I entered into a narrow dark tunnel where I started flying at the speed of a jet. It was indescribably frightening not because of the darkness in the narrow confines of the tunnel or the unbelievable speed. I feared the unknown world.

The only relief—which was of tremendous help—was the appearance once in a while of luminous beings on the tunnel walls. They would welcome, greet and console me through their vibrations. They only had or I could only see the upper half of a body. It was like I knew them from before. My knowledge of them was complete. They all had more or less the same type of vibration. Our communication was not disturbed by my speed.

Finally the tunnel was over and I saw the opening to a lighted area. I stepped onto a limitless desert and waited for an order (even my decision to wait was an order). Obviously this was the Court, the simplest and the most grand one. Later I was amazed by its self-sufficiency, perfection and speed. Quietly and without prelude, all my life appeared on a screen. All events from the very negligible to the most dramatic were being questioned and answered. Amazingly, but naturally, the screen was my own heart. Both the questions and the answers came from inside myself. The judge, the prosecutor, the attorney and the defendant were all me! The camera had recorded expertly every second of my life scenario. Events were so magnified that there was no way to mistake or misjudge. In some cases my value judgment was totally different from what I had in the world.

Watching the screen I could witness how my being was connected to other beings. It was as if we were all swimming in the same ocean. I saw how powerful and just and omnipresent the Judge is. Finally, I was sad because of my mistakes in the world and not having perfected myself before this judgment.

When the judgment came to an end—and it only took half a minute, I sat there waiting for the results. Suddenly I was ordered to leave the Court. I found myself back in the tunnel once more. I felt I was returning to the world. I was not happy to leave that place. I had gotten used to it, to its freedom and lightness.

On my way back I was not scared and the trip was shorter. I entered my office from the same spot on the ceiling. In a few seconds every attachment, responsibility and worldliness entered into my light form. My daughter was the first one to welcome me. I saw my physical being still sitting on the chair behind the desk, head down. I entered into my body, but when I became conscious, I found myself again in my room, face on the Quran. It was evening and time to break the fast. The whole episode had lasted about seven minutes. It was a serious taste of death which was more than enough for the rest of my life. It was a shock but I also felt extremely happy that there was still sometime left to take care of my real shortcomings. I thought I had gotten the point and could start this right away. However, after a few days I found that my new dilemma of how and where to start was even more confusing. It was like I could see the road but was unable to find the ramp. Time was passing fast just like cars pass you on a highway.

HAJJA NAZIHE

I learned many things from my father in [his first] seclusion. I experienced his forty days giving him the seclusion soup that my mother made for him [when I was six years old]. He ate it once every twenty-four hours and I gave him water because he had to perform the bath ablution five times a day before every prescribed prayer. I would hear from the next room that he was speaking to someone. When we returned to Damascus and Grandshaykh after the seclusion, Grandshaykh told me that my father had had conversations with angels. There he had been given his trust, his secrets from the Prophet through the angels and that he now has two angels always with him, following him. They stand beside him like lions.

One time I entered my father's room of seclusion during the last forty days of his seclusion and saw two lions in the room. I was afraid and ran away. During the forty days we saw lights coming from that room. At that time, thirty-five years ago, there was no electricity in that city. We used candles or kerosene lamps. One day we saw light coming from the room as if there were sunlight.

At that time when I was six I did not understand what my father was doing. I would get very hurt because my father did not speak to us for forty days, while he was speaking to someone in the room. We did not see him for forty days. How is it that he does not see us, but he sees someone else in the room. I did not know then that they were angels.

Part IV:
Conclusion

This brings to a close the story of seven Sufi women whose psychological profiles match those delineated by Shah Waliullah. Yet these women are themselves very much part of the edge of the 21st century, many as single parents, working, studying, teaching and fulfilling the trust of life bestowed upon them. Their stories differ from those of women who accept God's Will but do not commit themselves to inner change.

The second kind of women studied here are women who have both accepted submission to God's Will and commitment to inner change. They neither feel oppressed nor discriminated against as women. They realize it was actually their own egos which oppressed them and made them accept gender discrimination, itself a state of moral imbalance. With the acceptance of submission to God's Will and commitment to inner change, they have succeeded to a certain extent in overcoming ego—the satanic forces within—thereby liberating their conscience so that it can with certain conviction counsel self and others to perform what is right and prevent what is wrong. They each in their own way become activists who struggle against moral imbalance or injustice whether directed towards themselves or towards others.

Sufi Women
Hajja Nazihe

I learned patience from my mother when I was very young because my mother was very patient. She used to serve hundreds of people food daily in her home. She woke before the dawn prescribed prayer. After that prayer, she began cooking to feed all the people. She had to wash all the clothes by hand in big tubs for the guests who stayed in the mosque. I helped my mother. All of this was done for God's satisfaction.

My mother never complained to her husband or me about all the cooking and washing of clothes. When my maternal grandparents moved to Damascus, they lost all of their money. Maulana Shaykh Nazim had sold everything that he had and given it to Grandshaykh so they did not have extra money. Since my father worked for the people and for the religion of submission to God's Will, he did not have an income. My mother listened to her husband as a good wife does and as a disciple listens to a shaykh. She kept the respect of the shaykh as a shaykh and as a husband. Many times the shaykh did things which could not be explained, but she never complained. Even though her husband spent all his time with others, giving attention to the people, she never said anything. Now I am experiencing the same thing with Shaykh Hisham, not complaining, not objecting because Shaykh does not give me time....

LATIFA

Many women have also undergone seclusion in the Naqshbandi Order as Hajji Nazihe told me but it is typically when they are older, when they are less bound by demands and responsibilities. These responsibilities also go a long way to help women deal with their egos—child rearing, taking care of husbands, these very self-effacing tasks which is the point of what we are doing. She was saying that the seclusion of women is often easier than that of men. It is much less strenuous on them. Raising children and so forth is a kind of putting yourself last that serves one well. Half the religion is marriage and by extension is family and that is the biggest job that there is. It is something that two people do together but the burden of responsibility rests on the woman. There is an art to that. There is an art to bringing up the next generation. It is not the most difficult thing in the world to sit at prayer hour after hour but to do it with love and with humility, cleaning the toilets, cleaning dirty bums, washing dishes, doing laundry, doing all these things and not complaining.

As they express it, the role of woman is enhanced by Sufism. There is no sense of woman being inferior. Hajja Nazihe was given permission by Grandshaykh Abdullah al-Daghestani to initiate and lead the remembrance of God service for women, a service exactly the same as that performed by men. Latifa leads a woman's remembrance of God service. Khadija was initiated by a woman. Hoda leads groups of women and is married to a shaykh of the Naqshbandi Order, while Bagha experienced the egoless state. Rasheedah and Aliya each mention a dream which led them to commitment to inner change:

KHADIJA

Before this I had felt that I had accepted submission to God's Will outwardly in outer track, in dress, the headpieces, really adorned in modest attire but my heart was not clean. I would still backbite. I would still talk about people. Really it had not changed my heart. Since coming to Shaykh Nazim I have changed my attitude, changed my heart, become a calmer person. I used to be afraid of things. My faith was not as strong. I used to care about money and about material things. Following shaykh and doing my spiritual practices has made me very calm. I have even gotten down to eighteen cents in my wallet and not been afraid when, praise belongs to God, some one knocked at my door and bought me food. I have learned to push myself to the limit with faith and trust in God.

RASHEEDAH

After years and years of [searching for the way of inner commitment] I got so frustrated in searching in this way that I asked God Almighty if it be His will that I find the

Naqshbandi shaykhs that He make the way for me to do so, that I would just kind of let go and let God, as it were, do it.

BAGHA

Reading Sufi literature and being with a real Sufi shaykh has been a blessing to me. True shaykhs are all offering us the authentic jewel, but where is the one who can know and keep it?

As Hafiz, the Persian poet, says,

Between the lover and the beloved there is no veil
Hafiz you yourself are your own veil. Rise from in
 between.

Another poem called 'Black,' truly echoes our cry for our lost realm of happiness. The story of our trip to the alien planet of the world is superbly expressed. When finally we reach the point that we only like black, we are ready to dive in the ocean of annihilation and yield to the ecstasy of closeness to God. And to God belongs all success.

ALIYA

Even before I found Maulana Shaykh Nazim I asked God for a guide. In my heart, even verbally, I was saying, 'I know there is someone who knows the religion, who believes it, who practices it, who is a good living example of it. I was asking for that guide to come. I remember having a dream prior to meeting my friends from Cyprus in which I saw a very bright light. I was in a rural setting where the vegetation was very big and green and it had been divided off into plots where from one garden to the next garden, leaves were growing. It looked more Mediterranean than Western. This is the site that I saw in the dream but the light was there also. There was an intense joy. I felt so happy in this dream. I cannot explain the happiness or the brightness and the ease and the peace. Someone was calling to me in the dream, 'Are you going to

Friday congregational prayer? Are you going to Friday congregational prayer?'

I was said, 'Yes. I will be coming later. I am coming.'

Then I remember waking from the dream and feeling very happy, happier than I had felt in months. I had undergone a very ugly second divorce and this was so special to feel then. I remember feeling, 'There must be a guide. There must be someone who knows.' I remember I even made attempts to call people whom I thought were knowledgeable about the way of submission to God's Will, but I could never get through for some reason. There were Afro-American prayer leaders or scholars I was trying to reach. Somehow I never was able to find them. They were busy or they were away. I never gave up searching. I knew that it was out there. I knew that it would be in the form of an older man. I kept saying an older man, someone who has the signs of wisdom. It was shortly thereafter that my friends from Cyprus introduced me to Maulana Shaykh Nazim. They said, 'Have you heard of Maulana?'

I said, 'Yes, I think I have.' I remembered reading a copy of the newsletter which was at that time published out of Fenton, Michigan, "The Way of the Heart," where they had printed an association by Maulana Shaykh Nazim and a picture of him. I remember reading it over and over again in the mosque and then shortly thereafter I met the people from Cyprus and then everything began to fall into place.

NOTES

1 Shaykh Hisham Kabbani, "Debate on the Internet," p. 30.
2 Gisella Webb, "Sufism in America," in *America's Alternative Religions*, p. 249.
3 Javad Nurbakhsh, *Sufi Women*, pp. v-vii.
4 Shah Waliullah, *Altaf al-Quds*, pp. 5-6.
5 *Op. cit.*, pp. 34-35.
6 *Op. cit.*
7 *Op. cit.*
8 *Op. cit.*
9 *Op. cit.*
10 *Op. cit.*
11 *Op. cit.*, pp. 34-35.
12 *Op. cit.*, p. 16.
13 *Op. cit.*. p. 34.
14 *Op. cit.*
15 *Op. cit.*
16 *Op. cit.*
17 *Op. cit.*., p. 33.
18 *Op. cit.*
19 *Op. cit.*
20 *Op. cit.*
21 The Naqshbandi Sufi order is a traditional Sufi order which is the fastest growing Sufi order in America. The name means "imprinters," the goal being to imprint God's Most Beautiful Names on the spiritual heart.
22 Shah Waliullah, *Altaf al-Quds*, p. 28.
23 *Op. cit.*, p. 28.
24 *Op. cit.*, p. 30.
25 *Op. cit.*
26 *Op. cit.*, p. 31.
27 *Op. cit.* pp. 26-27.
28 *Op. cit.*, p. 23.
29 *Op. cit.*, p. 24.
30 *Op. cit.*, p. 33.
31 *Op. cit.*, pp. 25-26.
32 *Op. cit.*
33 *Op. cit.*, pp. 26-27.

BIBLIOGRAPHY

Bakhtiar, Laleh. *Moral Healer's Handbook: The Psychology of Spiritual Chivalry*, Vol. II of *God's Will Be Done*. Chicago: The Institute of Traditional Psychoethics and Guidance, 1994.

Bakhtiar, Laleh. *Moral Healing Through the Most Beautiful Names: The Practice of Spiritual Chivalry*, Vol. III of *God's Will be Done*. Chicago: The Institute of Traditional Psychoethics and Guidance, 1994.

Bakhtiar, Laleh. *Traditional Psychoethics and Personality Paradigm*. Vol. I of *God's Will Be Done*, Chicago: KAZI Publications, 1993.

Kabbani, Shaykh Muhammad Hisham. Debate on the Internet, 1992

Nurbakhsh, Dr. Javad. *In the Tavern of Ruins*: London: Khaniqahi Nimatullahi Publications, 1984.
Sufi Women. London: Khaniqahi Nimatullahi Publications, 1983.

Schimmel, Annemarie. *Mystical Dimensions of Islam*. Chapel Hill, NC: University of North Carolina Press, 1975.

Shah Waliullah. *Altaf al-Quds (The Sacred Knowledge.)* London: The Octagon Press, 1982. Changes in the text are by this author.

Webb, Gisela. "Sufism in America," in *America's Alternative Religions*, edited by Tim Miller. Albany: State University of New York Press, 1995.

A

Abiquiu, 19, 48
Africans, 26-27
Afro-American, 19, 24, 27, 31-32, 34, 46, 98
Ahmadiyya, 35
Al-din, 38
Al-hajj, 27
Al-hamid, 38
Al-haqqani, 40
Al-islam, 19, 48
Al-munkar, 19
Al-muslimeen, 36
Al-qadir, 38
Al-qubrusi, 46
Al-quds, 0, 66
Al-Shabbaz, 27
Allah, 18, 38, 47, 82
Amr, 19
Angel, 43-44
Angry, 8, 15, 60
Animality, 73
Animals, 11, 43, 66, 73
Ansar, 23
Apostate, 61
Aql, 41
Arabia, 26, 51-52, 96
As-Siddiq, 80
Avarice, 14
Ayesha, 52, 96-97

B

Backbite, 49, 95
Backbiting, 50, 65, 69
Baptist, 33, 35, 80-81
Baqa, 4
Bawa, 44-45
Brotherhood, 81
Brothers, 34, 79, 87
Buddhism, 40

C

Cactus, 87
California, 29
Chechnia, 38
Christ, 35, 81
Christian, 24-26, 35, 66, 81
Christianity, 25, 35, 40, 80
Clairvoyant, 41
Clement, 75
Compassion, 44, 74-75, 85
Concupiscent, 13
Counseling, 18, 71, 74
Creation, 72-73, 75-76
Creator, 58, 74-75
Cyprus, 46, 98

D

Daghestan, 38
Daghestani, 47
Damascus, 38-40, 77, 90, 94
Dante, 41
Darriah, 44
Dawud, 36, 68
Dhikr, 42, 50, 96-97
Disciple (s), 7, 44, 45, 47, 49, 52, 67, 79, 86, 94

E

Ecological, 11
Ecology, 9
Ecstasy, 97
Egocentricity, 72
Egoless, 72, 84, 95
Egos-child, 94
Egypt, 26, 52, 96
Elijah, 32-33
Envy, 49, 65
Eriteria, 24
Euro-American, 19

F

Faculties, 7, 9, 84
Faculty, 7, 9-10, 13, 63
Fitrat, 18
Friends, 18, 27, 33, 61, 77, 98
Friendship, 10, 31, 52, 60-61, 96

G

Gabriel, 3
Gambling, 60
Georgia, 24
Gospel, 33
Guardian (s), 43-44, 75

H

Habits, 43
Hafiz, 97
Hajji, 37, 50, 94
Haqq, 53
Haqqani, 51
Hope-fear, 73-74

I

Ill-tempered, 63
Imagination, 12, 27
Ishq, 41

J

Jamila, 53
Jesus, 23, 33, 35, 81
Jilani, 38
Jinn, 73

K

Kabah, 85
Kabbani, 3, 20, 45, 67, 99
Kamal, 38
Kathir, 3
Kazan, 38
Kedar, 51-52, 95-96
Koran, 61

L

Lebanon, 68-69
Lustful, 8

M

Mahdi, 36
Makkah, 3
Malaysia, 47
Malcolm, 27, 32-33
Massachusetts, 44
Messiah, 36
Michigan, 19, 51, 98
Monotheists, 57
Montreal, 23
Morocco, 39

N

Nafs, 7
Nahy, 19
Naqshbandis, 38, 51
Nigeria, 25

O

Octagon, 99
Ottoman, 38
Oxford, 25

P

Paradigm, 99
Paradise, 8, 47, 68, 82
Patience, 43, 75, 79, 82, 93
Peckham, 46-47
Persona, 35
Philadelphia, 44-45

Q

Quarrelsomeness, 63
Quranic, 3, 44, 83, 85

R

Race, 6, 35, 54
Rahma, 48
Ramadan, 43, 53, 88
Rashid, 52-53, 96-97
Recklessness, 63
Reformation, 13, 72
Regression, 65
Relationship, 24, 31, 41, 78
Religions, 35, 39, 51, 81, 99
Repentance, 74-75
Repression, 65
Resistance, 57-58, 61
Resolve, 12, 73, 83
Retribution, 59

Revolution, 38
Rumi, 38
Russia, 38
Russian, 38
S
Sacred, 0, 76, 99
Saints, 79-80, 82
Salahuddin, 36
Satanic, 57, 64, 72, 93
Saul, 35, 81
Schimmel, 99
Segregation, 25
Self-confidence, 64
Self-deprecating, 64
Self-efface, 45
Self-effacement, 4, 78, 86
Self-effacing, 78, 94
Self-esteem, 64
Self-examination, 75-76
Self-examine, 76
Self-existing, 76
Self-expression, 30
Self-indulgent, 63
Self-preservation, 65
Self-preserving, 8
Self-purification, 4-6, 62, 71, 83
Self-regulating, 19
Self-respect, 63
Self-restraint, 63, 73-74
Self-sufficiency, 88
Selfish, 63
Selfishness, 49
Shamanism, 40
Sincerity, 29, 44, 75-76, 78
Sisterhood, 81
Sisters, 28, 33-34, 48, 70, 79, 83, 87
Slavery, 32
Socialization, 57, 96
Sovereign, 74
Species-preserving, 8, 63

Spectacular, 50
States, 25, 36-37, 62, 64, 96
Station, 4, 43
Status-enhancing, 60
Stay, 41, 43, 87
Subliminal, 7
Sultan, 38
Superiority, 35
Supplication, 87
T
Tarsus, 35, 81
Tazkiyya, 3
Timidity, 16
Tradition, 3, 5, 36, 58, 66, 78
Traditions, 3, 9, 34, 39, 54
Transformation, 4
Trinidad, 23
Trinity, 23
Trustworthy, 10
Tsar, 38
Tyranny, 32
U
Ugly, 98
Unassertive, 64
Unbearable, 30
Unbelievable, 47, 88
Unbounded, 67
Uncharitable, 78
Universal, 75
V
Vain, 63
Valley, 43
Value, 17, 89
Vibration, 88
Vigilance, 74-75
Vigilant, 44, 75
W
Waqhia, 88
Z
Zeal, 14

OTHER WORKS BY THIS AUTHOR

AHADITH FOR CHILDREN (EDITOR). KAZI PUBLICATIONS, 1995.
ENCYCLOPEDIA OF ISLAMIC LAW: A COMPENDIUM OF THE MAJOR SCHOOLS (ADAPTER). KAZI PUBLICATIONS, 1995.
HAJJ: REFLECTIONS ON ITS RITUAL (TRANSLATOR). ABJAD, 1992.
IQBAL: MANIFESTATION OF THE ISLAMIC SPIRIT (TRANSLATOR). ABJAD AND OPEN PRESS HOLDINGS, 1991.
ISLAMIC MODEST DRESS: HIJAB (TRANSLATOR). KAZI PUBLICATIONS, 1993.
MORAL HEALER'S HANDBOOK: THE PSYCHOLOGY OF SPIRITUAL CHIVALRY. VOL. 2: GOD'S WILL BE DONE (AUTHOR). THE INSTITUTE OF TRADITIONAL PSYCHOETHICS AND GUIDANCE, 1994.
MORAL HEALING THROUGH THE MOST BEAUTIFUL NAMES: THE PRACTICE OF SPIRITUAL CHIVALRY. VOL. 3: GOD'S WILL BE DONE (AUTHOR). THE INSTITUTE OF TRADITIONAL PSYCHOETHICS AND GUIDANCE, 1994.
MUHAMMAD'S COMPANIONS: ESSAYS ON SOME WHO BORE WITNESS TO HIS MESSAGE (AUTHOR). KAZI PUBLICATIONS, 1993.
QURAN FOR CHILDREN (EDITOR). KAZI PUBLICATIONS, 1995.
RAMADAN: MOTIVATING BELIEVERS TO ACTION: AN INTERFAITH PERSPECTIVE (EDITOR). THE INSTITUTE FOR TRADITIONAL PSYCHOETHICS AND GUIDANCE, 1995.
RELIGION VS. RELIGION (TRANSLATOR). ABJAD, 1991.
SENSE OF UNITY: THE SUFI TRADITION IN PERSIAN ARCHITECTURE (CO-AUTHOR). UNIVERSITY OF CHICAGO PRESS, 1971.
SUFI EXPRESSIONS OF THE MYSTIC QUEST (AUTHOR). THAMES AND HUDSON, 1976.
TRADITIONAL PSYCHOETHICS AND PERSONALITY PARADIGM. VOL. 1: GOD'S WILL BE DONE (AUTHOR). INSTITUTE OF TRADITIONAL PSYCHOETHICS AND GUIDANCE, 1993.

RELATED BOOKS

Al-Ghazali on Disciplining the Soul and on Breaking the Two Desires.
Book of Sufi Healing.
Dreams and Their Meanings in the Old Arab Tradition.
Early Mystic of Baghdad.
Ethical Philosophy of al-Ghazali.
Ethical Theories of Islam.
Ethical Viewpoint of Islam.
Freedom from the Self.
Ghazali's Theory of Virtue.
Health Concerns for Muslims.
Ibn Seerin's Dictionary of Dreams.
Idea of Personality in Sufism.
Imam Razi's Ilm al-Akhlaq.
Islamic Medical Ethics in the Twentieth Century.
Islamic Perspectives in Medicine: A Survey of Islamic Medicine: Achievements and Contemporary Issues.
Majnun: The Madman in Medieval Islamic Society.
Medieval Islamic Medicine.
Milatti Islami: Islamic Treatment for the Disease of Addiction.
Moral Healing.
Muslim Character.
Muslim Tradition in Psychotherapy.
Natural Healing with Tibb Medicine: Medicine of the Prophet.
Psychology of Sufism.
Satan's Tragedy and Redemption: Iblis in Sufi Psychology.
Sufism and Psychology.
Sufism, Islam and Jungian Psychology.
Throne Carrier of God: The Life and Thought of Ala ad-Dawla as-Simnani.
Traditional Healer's Handbook.
Way of Sufi Chivalry.
Wiles of Women/ Wiles of Men. Joseph and Potiphar's Wife in Ancient Newar Eastern, Jewish and Islamic Folklore.

**The above titles are available at
KAZI Publications, Inc.**